Victorian Splendour

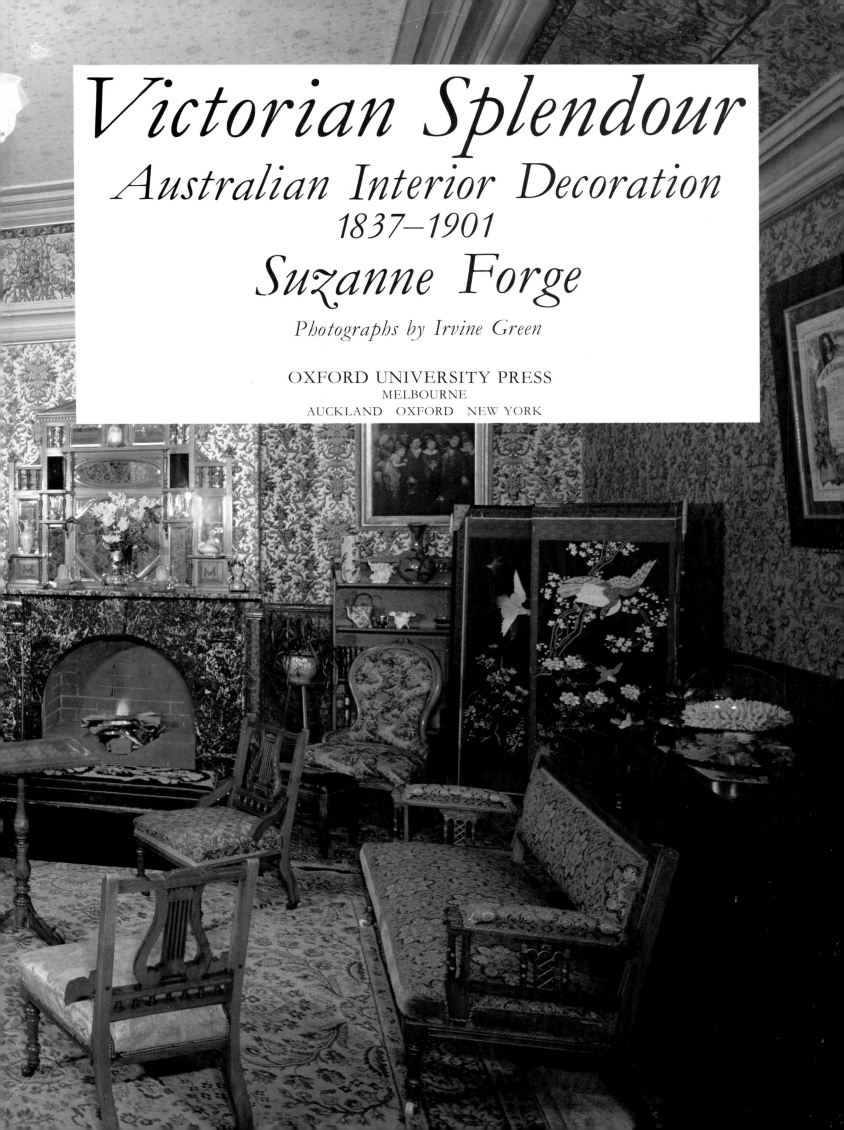

Victorian Splendour
Australian Interior Decoration
1837–1901
Suzanne Forge

Photographs by Irvine Green

OXFORD UNIVERSITY PRESS
MELBOURNE
AUCKLAND   OXFORD   NEW YORK

For my father.

ACKNOWLEDGEMENTS

EXPLANATIONS, DIRECTIONS, CLUES, PHOTOGRAPHS, research material, advice and encouragement—all freely and generously given—have greatly assisted me with this project. I am especially grateful to Dr Miles Lewis for his supportive and instructive role and to his wife, Mary, for her assistance at the La Trobe Library; also to Clive Lucas for his interest and painstaking checking of the manuscript, David Sheedy, Ian and Maisy Stapleton for their help in exploring Sydney interiors, and John Morris, Peter James and staff of the National Trust of Australia (New South Wales) for their jolly assistance. Likewise, I owe much to the National Trusts of Victoria, South Australia and Tasmania, especially Peter Watts of Melbourne, Frank Duffy of Launceston and Mrs Libby Hay of Hobart. I also thank the LaTrobe Library, Melbourne, and the State Library of Queensland for permission to reproduce photographs and other material from their collections, and Charles Cullis-Hill for photographs of Tudor Lodge from a family album.

I am profoundly grateful to my husband, Warwick, for his patience and support, as well as for the help he has given as a sounding board and manuscript reader. My children I thank too for their sweet affection and endurance of scant attention while the book was in preparation.

I count it among my greatest blessings to have worked with Irvine Green on this book. He has brought the benefit of his excellence as a photographer, his love of history and the pleasure of his company to the exercise. I am also tremendously grateful to Sue Goudie for her herculean typing performance, cheerfully rendered at all times, to Barbara Beckett for her splendid design work, and to Maggie Weidenhofer for her sympathetic editing.

My debt to the occupants of the many houses I have visited is vast. The magic of seeing such houses, and the wonderful hospitality offered to me, has made these visits unforgettable. Nor can I forget the dozens of people who have urged me on my way. Affection, inspiration and support have fostered the necessary spirit in me to last the distance.

S.F.

Front cover: The drawing-room at Mandeville Hall, Toorak, Victoria, with its adjoining conservatory.

Back cover: Elaborate stencilled decoration and paintwork enhances the cornice and ceiling of the dining-room at The Acacias, Marryatville, Adelaide, now the Loreto Convent.

Endpaper: A mid-Victorian dado paper reflects the Japanese influence on design.

Title page: The drawing-room at Navarre Station in Victoria was an extravagant addition to the original homestead, known as Heifer Station, which was built in 1857.

Page six and seven: Victorian taste translated into the Queensland idiom at Gracemere, near Rockhampton. The homestead was built by the Archer family in 1858 from ironbark slabs and bunya pine gathered on the property. Portraits of Archer pioneers Charles, William and Colin and their parents, William and Julia, hang on the walls.

Created and Produced by
Mead & Beckett Publishing
139 Macquarie Street Sydney for
Oxford University Press

Oxford London Glasgow
New York Toronto Melbourne Auckland
Nairobi Dar Es Salaam Cape Town
Kuala Lumpur Singapore Jakarta Hong Kong Tokyo
Delhi Bombay Calcutta Madras Karachi

First published November 1981
Reprinted February 1982

Forge, Suzanne
Victorian Splendour—Australian Interior
   Decoration 1837–1901
ISBN 0 19 554299 1.
1. Interior decoration—Australia—History—19th century. I. Title.
747.2'048

Photographs by Irvine Green
Designed by Barbara Beckett

Typeset by B & D Modgraphic, Adelaide
Printed by Toppan Printing, Hong Kong
Published by Oxford University Press, 7 Bowen Crescent, Melbourne.

Contents

Preface

THIS BOOK IS THE OUTCOME OF MY SEARCH for the true spirit of decoration in the Victorian era. It is a search that began with the acquisition of a Victorian house some ten years ago. To do the fine old house justice, I felt I had to understand what it was that motivated Victorians in the design and decoration of their houses. Why did they have such elaborately decorated rooms? What inspired their decorative motifs? Why did they use imitative techniques such as wood-graining? Was there a typical style of decoration? Why was a room decorated with a variety of bands, borders and friezes? How would our house have looked originally? How was the whole plan of decoration conceived and executed?

The answers to these questions and many others took a long time to unravel and led me through many fascinating byways. At the outset, I was dismayed by the scoffing, snorting twentieth-century attitude to the Victorians. Penetration of Victorian decoration seemed hardly to have gone further than to say they thrived on clutter, gloom and chasing dust. It fell far short of explaining the subtleties of colour, the richness of wallpaper and the delicacy of stencilling I had seen. Nowhere could I find a really favourable opinion of Victorian interiors; they seemed doomed to be regarded as some kind of aberration, only fit to be dismantled and recycled. I felt I had to get under the veneer of the period, past the tide of adverse opinion to discover for myself its fundamental impulses.

Many books, journals, magazines and newspapers of the period provided nineteenth-century opinion and advice on decoration. I learned that decoration was not a matter to be taken lightly—that rooms were not a careless mix of unrelated elements made more ludicrous by a profusion of meaningless bric-a-brac. Instead, great thought was given to the selection of an appropriate style for each room and a predominant hue with harmonizing and contrasting colours, and furnishings to complement the basic decorative elements. Very little was left to chance and even less to poor craftsmanship. Pride in the decorative arts and trades was very high and the general standard of work outstandingly impressive.

Old photographs of interiors, some showing their proud owners, are richly evocative of the period and proved an excellent source for the more transitory elements of rooms. Items such as drapes, curtains, table arrangements, carpets and such are best studied from these photographs.

In far-flung locations were a handful of houses that revealed to me original, unspoilt, unalloyed Victorian interiors. From hessian-lined cottages to silk-lined mansions, a tale unfolded of resourcefulness, ingenuity, subtlety and sheer beauty. From house to house a picture emerged of infinite variety and complexity. Such care had been lavished on even the humblest cottages, such lovely harmonies of pattern and colour were created. Far from being a tableau of routine treatments, Victorian decoration showed itself to be fundamentally artistic and vital.

The modest intention of this book is to reveal something of the skill,

An old lady sitting amid a sea of fascinating objects.

knowledge and spirit of the Victorian decorators and designers. By way of the surviving examples, readers will see for themselves the richness of the Victorian decorator's palette in Australia and savour the beauties of wallpapers, stencilling and the other decorative techniques.

The remarkable existence of these rooms after a century or more is, in itself, a cause for celebration. Some have suffered minor alterations, such as the conversion to electric light; others have some scars inflicted by careless twentieth-century hands. Most suffer from the deprivation of their original furniture, pictures, drapes and personal knick-knacks. However, despite these minor problems, the decorative character of each room shines through and the appropriateness of the decoration to the room is at once apparent. Lamentably, few of these houses are on view to the public and those that are tend to be of the grand variety. Middle-class and working-class houses have been included in this book to broaden the range of examples.

Victorian rooms, stripped of their embellishments, are a sorry sight. Lofty walls, spacious ceilings and elaborate architectural detail cry out for complementary decorative treatments, especially the division of surfaces into sub-sections such as the dado filling and frieze. Otherwise, walls yawn vacantly and ceilings droop in sad suspension. The chapters devoted to the techniques of decoration are intended to explain how they were used in Victorian rooms. Examples illustrated in this section are from rooms rehabilitated by new owners and treated to a sympathetic decorative scheme.

I hope that this book engenders in others the pleasure in Victorian interiors that I have developed while researching the subject. Especially, I hope that the few precious houses that have survived the march of time will be enjoyed and appreciated by all of us as well as by future generations of Australians.

SUZANNE FORGE
Melbourne
1981

Introduction

Re-establish the natural harmony of things, after science and business, art; after work, recreation or rest; after calling on the positive activity of reasoning, let the dreaming imagination and the heart's feelings soar; after the true and the utilitarian, invoke the beautiful; and well-being will come abundantly to you, with health of body and soul.[1]

IF WE ARE TO ENJOY AND APPRECIATE Victorian interiors we must first understand the Victorian attitude towards decoration. The Victorians had a passion for ornament. That is not to say they applied it indiscriminately. They thought it was natural, necessary, civilized, enjoyable and positively elevating. By means of ornamentation they believed any object could be improved, if not transformed. There was no limit to the joys and benefits of decoration. It was asserted that by the application of decorative art 'a very barn may become a palace'.[2] They believed in the inherent need to ornament, deducing from the simple daubings of savages that, even at his most primitive, man had an undeniable desire to ornament himself and his surroundings, to make himself as attractive as possible. With dazzling logic, they calculated that their advanced civilization, with all its splendid achievements, could be expected to produce a feast of ornamentation. In fact anything less than a major commitment to ornament was inexcusable. Without it, 'the mind must revolt at a mere crude utility', it was said in 1851.[3]

In the Georgian and Regency periods, by comparison, a simpler decorative order prevailed. Both architectural forms and decorative treatments were more restrained, largely due to the limitations imposed by their mode of manufacture, that is, hand-crafted work. Colour, however, was applied with considerable boldness. Rich reds, greens, deep golds and blues were used to splendid effect, along with the pastels, creams and whites that are more readily associated with the pre-Victorian period. The so-called heavy Victorian colours were not so much a novelty as was the elaborateness of the schemes in which they were employed in the Victorian period. Early Victorian houses such as Elizabeth Bay House, Sydney, reveal much of the pre-Victorian taste for simple yet strong decoration.

With an extroverted enthusiasm, revelling in their freshly acquired opportunities to extend the boundaries of decoration, the Victorians adorned the exteriors and interiors of their buildings with a variety of embellishments. They felt no need to curb their pleasure in ornament any more than we would feel the need to curb our pleasure in laughter or music. Nor were there any inhibitions about the display of beautiful objects and the demonstration of material success. Modesty in such matters did not seem to earn any particular esteem. Admiration was more readily obtained by doing well and showing one's success to the world. The pressure of competition was keenly felt. 'The age is one of competition, one

A vivid use of colour and an unusual ceiling strike a bold note in this modest family sitting-room at Merigal, Nowra, New South Wales. Two shades of green, echoing the wallpaper colours, are used in the woodwork to bind the room into a cohesive decorative entity. A mellow old carpet consolidates the effect.

11

Shreds of a picket fence stand sentinel around this cottage near Newstead, Victoria, while old roses climb up over the roof. Within, the walls are lined with hessian and carry sections of colourful Victorian wallpapers (page 74).

Eeyeuk, Victoria, built c. 1859. This two-roomed cottage was the home of Alexander Dennis and family for some years, before the grand bluestone house of 1875 was constructed. A shingle roof lurks beneath the galvanized iron. Inside, its walls are lined with hessian hung with pretty floral wallpaper (page 23).

of rivalry' confided an anonymous writer in 1887. In a time of unprecedented social mobility, it was imperative to stake one's claim on the social ladder. There were no prizes for reticence. On the whole, they saw no harm in an abundance of decoration provided it was executed, in their opinion, with taste and intelligence. Decoration was regarded as an art of great significance, worthy of profound analysis and endeavour.

Questions of style, taste, form, ornament and colour were pondered seriously. Men such as John Ruskin, A. W. Pugin, Owen Jones, Christopher Dresser, William Morris, Bruce Talbert and Lewis Day dwelt with intellectual gravity on the development of architecture and the decorative arts in the second half of the nineteenth century. While the need for ornament was accepted more or less without question by all, its precise application was a matter for earnest thought. There was no place for the frivolous, the haphazard or the flimsy. 'In household furnishings, baldness is as undesirable as flimsiness'.[4] Instead, a great deal of care was devoted to every aspect of decoration at all levels. Middle-class householders were given ample direction on how to decorate their rooms, as well as how to run the household, in books such as *Cassell's Household Guide* and in newspaper articles and magazines. Publications abounded, particularly from the mid-Victorian period onward. Many books were published on furnishing and decoration, such as Charles Eastlake's *Hints on Household Taste*, which appeared in 1878, and Bruce Talbert's *Examples of Ancient and Modern Furniture, Metal Work, Decorations etc.* in 1876.

The importance of Taste in all decoration was the subject of numerous treatises. Educated taste was the ideal—a combination of a thorough knowledge of all aspects of decoration, including the historic, with a certain sense of what was appropriate. In this latter respect the attainment, in decoration, of the qualities of harmony and repose was all-important. No room could be considered a decorative success unless it could be said to possess these subtle effects. In Victorian texts the words harmony and repose were frequently used to establish standards of decoration.

The attainment of repose is the highest aim of art. Repose cannot be found if forms are apparent which betoken ignorance, vulgarity, or coarseness. The eye will rest on a surface which reveals beauties of form, harmonies of colour, knowledge on the part of the decorator, and which has an absence of crude and garish qualities, and it will there find repose . . . the highest sense of repose—i.e. dreamy, soothing repose, may be realised where the brightest colours are employed. Repose is attained by the absence of any want. A plain wall of dingy colour reveals a want; it does not then supply all that is necessary to the production of a sense of quiet and rest. A wall may be covered with the richest decoration, and yet be of such a character that the eye will rest upon it and be satisfied . . . We must always remember that repose is compatible with richness, subtlety, and radiance of effect.[5]

Harmony referred specifically to the art of combination in decoration. To skilfully blend elements with sufficient, but not excessive, contrast to achieve an effect that was exciting and yet pleasing, was the ultimate goal of decoration. If a room combined elements of one basic theme but successfully admitted variety and contrast to that theme, then it could be said to possess the elusive but ideal quality of harmony. Owen Jones wrote in 1851: 'The secret of success is the production of a broad general effect by the repetition of a few simple elements, variety being sought rather in the arrangements of the several portions of the design than in the multiplication of varied forms.'[6] Following this approach, the elements of a room would derive from a few motifs of a particular origin, perhaps classical, floral, geometric or something else, which could be used in a number of ways. The description of a typical mid-Victorian drawing-room indicates the significance of harmony in the decorative scheme: 'Beginning with this rich carpet with its sober tints, the eye ascends to the dado, to the walls, to frieze, cornice and ceiling, and finds variation at every stage, but no break in the harmony of all.'[7]

The part played by colour in Victorian decoration was most significant. Ornamentation and the highly developed use of colour formed the decorative hallmark of the age. It was once remarked that the Victorians saw themselves as coming to the rescue of a world deprived of pattern and colour. Clearly their response to the new potential of pattern and colour in decoration was exuberant. They understood the technology of colour perfectly and made a brilliant success of its use in design and decoration.

They made a minor science of colour and its reproduction in all areas of technology. Colours were analysed theoretically and studied for their various effects and interrelationships. The complexities of colour became one of the specialities of the Victorian period, a superb range being developed for use in the textile, printing and decorating fields. In decoration, carpets, wallpapers and fabrics were the products of highly complicated colour technology calling for large numbers of colours. By today's standards, it seems there was an astonishingly high level of appreciation of the nuances of colour. The ability to combine colours successfully seems to have been widely accomplished and is also evidenced in arts such as costume-design, embroidery and porcelain-painting as well as interior decoration. The high level of craftsmanship and skill in the decorating trades may account for the achievement of successful colour-schemes in part, though perhaps it was an aspect of life better understood by the Victorians than ourselves. The art of colour-combination was more seriously cultivated then than it is today. It was not uncommon to find as many as twelve colours combined successfully in the floor and wall decoration of one room. Decorators were practised at implementing polychromatic decorative schemes involving several wallpapers and stencilling in a single room.

Instructions on using colour in decoration emphasized the need for harmony:

It should be remembered that the 'colour' of an apartment may be mainly divided into four or five chief divisions or quantities. There are to be considered the ceiling, the walls, the floor covering, the drapery, the covering of the furniture, and, perhaps, the wood or material of the furniture itself. Everyone of these will have some effect upon, and, therefore should have some relation to all the others . . . do not have too much of one colour but vary it with something sufficiently unlike to prevent a glaring effect . . . the colours should neither stare at the beholder, nor quarrel with one another.[8]

The last injunction is most apposite. It shows clearly the desire to establish exactly the right degree of assertiveness for each colour. It expresses perfectly the fine line between a colour being so soft as to be ineffectual or so strong as to be aggressive. It demonstrates a sound knowledge of the effect of colour upon the beholder.

The foundations for this thorough understanding of the effects of colour were laid down by George Field in 1835 in his *Chromatography*, though there were comments on the use of colour in earlier books. His systematic analysis of all basic colours and their secondary and tertiary blends formed a solid basis on which Victorian colour-use could be laid. For most of the Victorian period, the attachment to tertiary colours gave Victorian decoration its reputation for heaviness. Rather than using primary colours which were avoided assiduously, they used a range of secondary colours, such as green and brown, which were then blended to create a greater number of closely related tertiary shades. The result was that while colours were a little subdued, they were free of the harsh jarring quality that characterizes much modern colouring. Analysis of the colour-composition of any particular decorative element of this period usually shows it to consist of basically soft, muted colours with here and there a dash of a more positive colour. Gold was also used extensively to highlight what might otherwise have been somewhat sombre colour-schemes. Altogether, the Victorians usually managed to combine colours, within a pattern, with dash, verve and apparent ease.

Typically compact, this late Victorian cottage in North Melbourne has a cosy parlour decorated with an impressive, original, large-scale wallpaper (page 38).

Navarre Station, near Ararat, Victoria, photographed c. 1890, reflects the typical stages of transition through which properties passed during the Victorian period. In the 1880s, the Kelleher family made fashionable improvements, including the creation of a splendid drawing-room (pages 6 and 7).

Unusual timber fretwork gives a nordic air to the façade of Belmont, at Raglan, Victoria, in this photograph taken in 1910 (page 34).

Painted in 1903, this view shows the romantic, mildly Gothic styling of Merigal, which was built in 1887 by a Scottish builder, Kenneth MacKenzie, for his family. Descendants still occupy the house, which retains much of its original decoration and furnishing.

They tackled the question of style, however, with a rather disarming naivety. Brimful of enthusiasm and spiritedness, they embraced a number of styles in a broad sweep. Sources of decoration as far-flung as Chinese and Moorish, Japanese and Greek were absorbed into the decorative consciousness of the nineteenth century. An outgoing approach and a pleasure in variety coloured the Victorian decorator's palette. As the Empire expanded and flourished, so too did the sentiment of global kinship. Past civilizations and distant cultures were all seen to blend into a cohesive harmonious entity, the Empire. Queen Victoria herself encouraged a belief in the fraternity of her dominions by having Indians in particular on her personal staff.

Exhilarated by the surge of industrialization and boosted by their accomplishments, the Victorians went into the second half of the nineteenth century on a wave of optimism. This is best demonstrated by the Great Exhibition of 1851, in which dozens of nations took part. In the awesome expanse of the Crystal Palace, the merging of distant cultures took place. Competing for technical and artistic supremacy were the most splendid, ingenious and elaborate products from each country. Not only was the industrial pace set for all participants, but the stage was set for a multi-cultural approach to decoration. It was not the first time an eclectic approach had been advocated. During the eighteenth century much attention was focused on the appeal of the exotic in architecture and landscape design. The building of the Great Pagoda in the Kew Gardens in 1761 by Sir William Chambers advertised the fascination of oriental gardens. In 1815 John Nash began the fabulous Brighton Pavilion for the Prince of Wales. With its exotic mixture of Indian domes, Islamic arches and minarets and Gothic elements, the Pavilion heralded the popular acceptance of the unorthodox in architecture and decoration. The idea of an eclectic style took root firmly in the early years of Victoria's reign, arising spontaneously from the excitement of exploration,

archaeology, travel and the stimulus of industry. As early as 1839, in *The Rudiments of Curvilinear Design*, George Phillips encompassed a wide range of styles including Gothic, French, Chinese, Grecian, Byzantine, Arabian and 'Hindoostanee'.

But by 1851 the voice of eclecticism was loud and clear. Why should a country with so much of beauty to choose from, limit herself to traditional sources of design? Why should decoration be starved in the confines of a conventional strait-jacket? Could a new all-embracing decorative style be evolved that incorporated the best of all previous styles both historic and contemporary? Among designers, an affirmative response to this challenge enabled an eclectic approach to blossom and subsequently to bear fruit for most of the century. Much of this tasty fare was carried far and savoured in distant colonies such as Australia, America and Canada.

The final blessing to this philosophy came from the scholarly Owen Jones in his *Grammar of Ornament* in 1854. His erudite analysis of all major sources of ornament, including that of Savage Tribes and Egyptian, Celtic and Renaissance civilizations, gave the seal of approval to the more exotic motifs, placing them side by side with the classics of Greece and Rome. He espoused 'an imaginative and intelligent eclecticism' as a viable and appropriate decorative philosophy for the nineteenth century.

It is to Jones's work on ornament then that we can trace the diversity of decorative elements in Victorian houses. The use of classical motifs as a basic style proved to be a highly successful formula, followed in Australia longer than in most other places. A heavy bias towards the Renaissance style, which, in turn, was derived from classical Greece, is shown in the exterior and interior of Australian houses of this period. For example the acanthus leaf, the chief motif of Corinthian architecture, was used widely. Among other uses, it was arranged to form the

A self-portrait of Charles Archer in his hut on Waroongundi station at Emu Creek, in Southern Queensland. He and his brother Tom built the hut in 1845. At this stage, only the essentials are in evidence. A primitive writing table provides a tenuous link with family and civilization, while the shot-gun and pistols are at hand. Such simply built, frugally furnished huts were often the starting point of a colonist's rise to affluence and the acquisition, by the mid-Victorian period, of a 'fine' house.

15

Gracemere at Rockhampton, Queensland, shows the low slung roofline and shady vegetation chosen by the Scottish Archer pioneers to protect them against the summer heat (pages 2 and 3).

Woolmers, established near Launceston in Tasmania by another branch of the Archer family is one of the few estates in the country to have retained its homestead complete with Victorian decorations and furnishings, as well as gardens, stables and outbuildings (pages 39, 54 and 58).

Looking remarkably like the work of the twentieth century, Pastoria, near Kyneton, Victoria, was remodelled extensively from 1892 to 1894. Mining millionaire John Boyd Watson, junior, was responsible for the modernization of the pioneer George Govett's modest conventional house. The interior has retained much of the decoration of this period (pages 18 and 27).

capital of the classical Corinthian column, which was a key element of Renaissance architecture. The Victorians adapted it for a wide variety of uses. Columns were shortened, lengthened, fattened or slimmed. They were covered with tracery and other embellishments and used on verandahs, entrance halls and other rooms. The same motif, the acanthus leaf, also found its way on to plaster cornices, corbels, ceiling roses and into trailing arabesque designs in glass, stencilling and wallpapers.

Following the same meandering course from the temples of ancient Greece to Victorian houses in Australia was the egg-and-dart design, which frequently formed the basis of frieze and cornice work. Varied frets such as the Greek key were also widely adopted by designers of the nineteenth century. These examples and the much stylized honeysuckle flower and the Egyptian papyrus and lotus flower formed the basic repertoire of motifs in Renaissance art from which the Victorians drew their inspiration.

A relatively fresh force, in architectural and decorative terms, was the Gothic style, which flourished in northern Europe in the thirteenth century. In the frenzy of architectural revivals that took place in the Victoria era, it was resuscitated by its great exponent, Pugin. In Australia many public buildings, especially churches and banks, were built in this style, by William Wardell in particular. A few houses, such as The Abbey at Annandale, Sydney, were built by Wardell's builder, John Young. Mostly the Gothic motifs stayed within the Gothic architectural context, forming a tight stylistic entity. The former E.S. and A. bank on the corner of Collins and Queen Streets in Melbourne is a perfect example of this fully integrated Gothic style. Wonderful stencilled and gilded work ornaments the architectural forms of the main banking chamber, and the residential quarters above.

The flexibility with which most other decorative motifs was used was considerable and it was not uncommon to find a Japanese or Indian room behind an Italianate façade. Within each room even greater licence was permitted. Motifs were mixed, matched and welded in a spirit of exuberant eclecticism.

This broad expansive attitude was still held by some in 1892. An English architect, Andrew Wells, on a visit to Australia in that year, told a group of architects:

Practically there is no limit to the mode of treatment for every part of the house, I am far from thinking there is only one good way of painting houses, there are many. For instance if character is wanted, the houses could be treated in purely Greek design, or Pompeiian, and they are beautiful designs . . . affording scope for full harmonious colouring. The Renaissance is founded on the Classic, but treated with abundant freedom and grace by the Italians and other European nations. The various French developments of the Renaissance have their own beauties—Louis Quinze, and Louis Seize are full of character, lightness and elegance.[9]

So for those who could afford it, it was a case of 'Pay your money and take your choice'. No embarrassment attached to eclecticism. If Victorian interiors are to be appreciated, it must be in this context, in this climate of opinion.

The effect of cross-pollination expressed itself in the Aesthetic movement of the 1870s and 1880s. Typically luscious swirling flowers, leaves and stems were woven into a web of classical arrangements and motifs with here and there a touch of exotic oriental asymmetry. A panoply of rich bold designs abounding in a kind of hybrid vigour reached the householder. Many quite exquisite floral motifs appeared. Some designers followed Ruskin's philosophy, that nature was perfection herself, and aimed at a faithful representation of nature. Others thought this pointless and 'adapted' or 'stylized' plants so that they were recognizable but not in a specific way. Flowing from this approach of Jones and Pugin was the 'conventionalizing' of nature, which Dresser encouraged greatly. He wished to represent nature in its 'ideal' art form, far from the irregularities and blemishes of nature in reality.

Simultaneously, the pioneers of the Arts and Crafts movement had been causing small ripples in the large pond of industrialized Britain since the 1870s. Ten years later their designs, if not their socialist philosophy, had earned them a small following. Much of their success was due to the leadership of Morris. A man of many talents, his work as a designer of textiles and papers was superbly fresh and original. The movement was promoted by architects Charles Voysey and Baillie Scott and by designers Walter Crane and Day. They espoused values of craftsmanship and artistic excellence, and established community workshops to counter the prevailing artificial and highly mechanized approaches of the factories. For artistic inspiration they turned to the mediaeval world with its unspoilt values, and to nature. Morris immersed himself in the fabric of nature, aiming for 'unmistakable suggestions of gardens and fields, and strange trees, boughs and tendrils.'[10] These men appreciated Japanese art, which had begun to capture the Victorians' imagination since a collection of Japanese pieces were first exhibited in 1862. Leading designers such as Dresser and Edwin Godwin made a serious study of Japanese art and were much taken with it. Arts and Crafts work had an idyllic, cottagey quality and a disposition towards Japanese asymmetry. Above all, it possessed a sweetness and naivety that did much to swing decoration away from its retrospective preoccupation towards something novel that later materialized in the form of Art Nouveau.

The development of diverse styles was very much related to the response to mechanization. A dramatic consequence of the 1851 Exhibition was the impetus it gave to spending and production. In an amazing display of technical virtuosity, goods were exhibited that opened the gates to a flood of fanciful styles and fantastic creations as well as everyday furniture. Without the restrictions of manufacture by hand, the possibilities of production were virtually limitless. Furniture-making, along with many other occupations, was transformed from a craftsman's trade to a vast manufacturing business. A feverish excitement caused by the unprecedented array of machine-made goods gave rise to an all-class shopping spree. Matching suites for dining-room, drawing-room, and bedroom were a huge success. Shapely carved styles had great appeal after the austerity of hand-made goods, especially for the less affluent householders who could afford few elaborate possessions in the pre-mechanized days. The acquisition of many showy possessions became associated with success and respectability.

Linked to this materialism was the Victorians' abhorrence of plainness and emptiness in a room. The tone of such a room could only serve to downgrade a person of any level in society. Meagre decoration and furnishing were synonymous with poverty and misery. Conversely, an aura of warm cosiness and personalized charm did much to enhance the home-owner in the eyes of society. The cultivation and expression of individuality in decoration was, in fact, much encouraged by Queen Victoria. An 1894 description of the drawing-room in the royal residence at Sandringham expresses the importance attached to the personality of a room.

We are looking into a room which is lived in, which is impressed with a personality; and such signs of individuality make the true value of decoration. Elegance by itself is not enough in a drawing room; the charm lies in that peculiar air which the possessor gives it, which enables us to see in it the fancy of its mistress, to feel her presence, and which thus makes it indeed a Presence Chamber. The charm is not easy to define. It does not arise only from the books and music here and there, the embroidery or sketches, the feather screens or painted china which discover the lady's skill and taste; it is rather in the whole atmosphere, the colours and the arrangement that the subtle influence reveals itself.[11]

Filled with a whole-hearted zest for the new machine-made products, the Victorians lavished on their houses as much rich-looking decoration as they could afford. What the millionaire could afford, the upper middle class aped. What their social inferiors could not equal in quality, they endeavoured to match in style.

Glenhope, at Pennant Hills, Sydney, was built in 1895 as the home of a citrus orchardist, Mr W. Salisbury, and his wife. The hall and drawing-room have been well preserved and reveal much of the contemporary style of decoration (pages 35 and 58).

One of the most extensively preserved examples of interior decoration in Australia is at Yallum Park, Penola, South Australia, which was built in about 1888.
(pages 50–51, 59, 67 and 78).

Notions of Gothic purity influenced builder John Young in the design of this house, The Abbey, and its neighbours, at Annandale, Sydney. Young had worked with William Wardell, the eminent architect in Sydney and Melbourne and was therefore steeped in the Gothic style. This photograph was taken in 1884. (pages 27 and 119).

Left: Pastoria, near Kyneton, Victoria. Well ahead of its time in architectural and decorative trends, this gallery cum sitting-room, was built as part of a major alteration between 1892 and 1894 by the magnate J. B. Watson. The room achieves a surprising informality with its generous use of natural timbers and plain inglenook fireplace. Richly embossed imitation leather wallpaper is hung on the walls of the upper level.

Above: Soft-hued wallpaper and cosy modesty pervade the drawing-room at Merigal. The floral pink and brown paper conveys essential lightness and femininity. A Victorian landscape of the Nowra district hangs above the piano. The narrow timber cornice is painted in shades of pink to harmonize with the walls, as is other joinery. Similarly, a complete cast-iron chimneypiece, not shown in the picture, is painted in shades of pink and cream. Original venetian blinds are hung in the windows.

Busily and beautifully eclectic—objects of interest from all quarters covered the walls of Tudor Lodge, the home of Mr Cullis-Hill in Harcourt Street, Hawthorn, near Melbourne, when it was photographed in 1891. It was said that 'The studios of Europe and the almost equally artistic showrooms of Gillows have been ransacked to decorate the walls, floors and ceilings.' The house was built in 1880–81.

An interesting basis for comparison is provided by this photograph of Gracemere, Rockhampton, at the turn of the century and the present-day photograph (pages 2 and 3). This early photograph shows the original chimneypiece and kerosene light-fitting and evokes the Victorian atmosphere well. Some early twentieth-century chairs are also in evidence.

And so it went on, all along the line, with the simple cottage-owner having a house with decoration that bore a distinct resemblance, in format, if not in quality or scale, to that of his superiors.

The imitative techniques were of the greatest assistance in facilitating this conformity to certain fashions. Wood-graining, marbling and stencilling made it possible for the appearance, at least, of the richest materials to be achieved. Wood-graining brought the lustre of prestigious timbers such as oak and mahogany to the middle-class home-owner. Marbling gave spectacular-looking combinations of the best marbles for the price of a mixture of paints and the services of a skilled tradesman. Stencilling brought the magnificence of hand-painting into the average home. Large tracts of wall and ceiling could be ornamented systematically and efficiently with impressive-looking designs.

Not all decorators advocated the use of such bogus and 'dishonest' techniques, and in fact many, such as Charles Eastlake, vehemently denounced them.[12] Their efficacy, however, was indisputable, and they made impressive effects available cheaply to masses of home-decorators. Ultimately, it seems, the imitative treatments asserted themselves as legitimate artistic techniques, and much finesse and variety were developed in their application.

Jones supported the use of imitations only where the use of the material imitated would not be inconsistent. He condoned the use of imitation marble, for instance, in a grand home where one might expect to find real marble, but disapproved of its use in a house of lesser grandeur, where the use of marble would be incongruous. It was not the artificiality of the process to which he objected, but rather its use as a weapon of social pretension.

Needless to say, the majority of people whose middle-class houses lacked solid materials were not deterred by this moral point of view. They were not going to have the real thing anyway, so why should they miss out on the imitation? The vast extent of wood-graining, in particular, indicates that the pervasive desire for attractive appearances successfully overcame any intellectual objections voiced by the artistic élite.

Whether one finds oneself attracted by the splendour of these imitative techniques or repelled by their false nature, one must accept that they formed an essential part of the spectrum of Victorian decoration. The complete decorative fabric with its many detailed and diverse elements was generally very much dependent on the implementation of one or more imitative or false treatments. A typical drawing-room, for instance, would be resplendent with items of papier mâché, silver plate, spelta (imitation bronze), gold-leaf, as well as the abundant veneered furniture and wallpaper.

The rest of the decorative scheme was filled by carpets, curtains, light-fittings, pictures, upholstered furniture and bric-a-brac. Combining these with surface decoration to achieve the desired effect was a talent cultivated keenly by the Victorian lady. A fine house was the greatest asset and all aspiring householders strove to make the house, no matter how small, as impressive as possible.

In 1892 Wells expressed it poetically:

I don't think there is a wiser way of spending money than in making the home beautiful. Our wives and families spend most of their lives at home, and the enjoyment derived from beautiful surroundings is beyond estimate, besides, the refining influence it has on our children, there is no pleasure so constant, so soothing, so lasting and elevating, as that afforded by a lovely home.[13]

Wallpapers, or wall-hangings as they were called, offered the Victorians some other excellent imitations. It was not uncommon to find granite, marble, oak, leather and carved stone represented on paper decorating the walls of large impressive houses as well as cottages. Wallpapers of an amazing diversity and ingenuity were available. Floral designs were extremely popular and were made with matching borders and friezes. Damasks, flocks, washable 'sanitaries' and other highly decorative types of papers were produced in reams.

It was a common practice to arrange several papers on the wall so as to divide it into three horizontal levels or divisions. At the base, above the skirting, was the dado of approximately a metre in height. It had a border or capping at the top to separate it from the main, infill section of the wall. The frieze, which could range from a narrow band to a half-metre deep, reached to the base of the cornice. The arrangement of the wall treatment into these three sections—dado, filling and frieze—was a basic formula revived from the architecture of Pompeii. It was varied often and carried out in painted and stencilled treatments as well as in wallpaper in most rooms. In the drawing-room, however, sometimes the dado was omitted. A variation on this arrangement was to divide the wall into panels in the style of Louis XIV decoration with wallpaper or stencilling filling the panels. This was fashionable in the early Victorian period and had waves of popularity in the Edwardian era.

Wallpapers were also used to decorate ceilings. Geometric designs served this function admirably. Alternatively, ceilings were often painted a pastel shade to harmonize with the wall colour and the cornices carried stencilled designs as ornamentation. Another decorative phenomenon of the Victorian period was the use of the elaborate plaster cornices and ceiling roses. The Georgians used hand-run timber and plaster cornices but these were somewhat narrower and plainer than the mass-produced Victorian examples.

As the decorative tempo increased towards the middle of Victoria's reign, architectural elements such as cornices, dados and mouldings generally became more pronounced, while the patterns in rooms became bolder and the colours richer. Houses built in the 1860s would therefore have less ornate architectural embellishments and decoration than those built in the 1880s. Plasterwork reflects this progression closely. Also, within a house, the relative elaborateness of cornices reflected the importance of each room, the drawing-room usually having more embellishments than other rooms. Many houses of a modest quality did not have moulded cornices and ceiling roses and often made do with a simple beading or a band of wallpaper at the junction of wall and ceiling. Even in grander houses, the plasterwork tended to peter out in minor bedrooms and was non-existent in service rooms.

However, where moulded plaster cornices and ceiling roses were present, they received careful and often very lavish decoration closely linked to the theme of the wall and ceiling decoration. Bands of colour, ranging from the darkest colour used in the wall decoration to the lightest colour in the ceiling, were used on the cornice, which served as a decorative link between the two planes. The rose was similarly coloured, though sometimes more dramatically, with a view to its being the ceiling centrepiece. Gilding of the outer portions of the cornice and ceiling rose, so that the gold picked up the light, was also conventional.

Painted work played a major part in all parts of decoration. In rooms that were either hung with wallpaper or stencilled, painted ceilings, cornices and joinery completed the decorative effect. Sometimes sections of wall were painted an appropriate harmonizing colour rather than being papered. This was not done in such a way as to give a plain or vacant effect, but to create an important element in the total scheme of decoration. Usually the main infill section was decorated in this way though there are also examples of painted dados.

Joinery, if it was not solid polished timber, which was rare, or wood-grained, was painted to harmonize with or highlight colours in the wall decoration. Usually two shades of a colour were used, the lighter shade being applied to the recessed panels of doors and skirtings and the darker covering the remaining portions. Two shades of soft green, brown, terracotta or pink might be used in such a way. Often extra highlighting was provided by a fine gold line on the angled edge of the mouldings. The panels of doors were given further embellishments of stencilling or floral designs, sometimes by the lady of the house.

The English style at its most grand is shown in this late-Victorian photograph of Queen Victoria's drawing-room at Sandringham. Clusters of chairs, crowded by palms and massive objets d'art *create an aura of intense interest and personalized charm.*

When Captain Weston left the Indian army to settle in New South Wales in 1831, he brought with him some Indian servants and some exotic customs. One servant, Ramdiall, used to sit on the back porch at mealtimes with the rope from the overhead punkah, shown here, between his toes, and by drowsily moving his leg, would swing the punkah and so create a breeze to cool the family. Captain Weston's house, Horsley, is shown with its early Victorian furniture and architectural detail.

The twentieth-century use of white paint would have shocked the Victorians. The seemingly irresistible use of white for walls, ceilings and joinery would have struck horror into their hearts. As a colour it was considered by them to be at best, expressionless, and at worst a treatment fit for a primitive pioneer slab hut or a pig-sty, not a drawing-room. With a few exceptions, its legitimate use in decoration was limited to a few fine lines or highlights either in wall decoration or cornice treatment until about 1895, when it emerged as a respectable colour for use in drawing-rooms in particular. Its main use was as a plain sterile treatment for outhouses and farm buildings. To use white, *en masse*, in decoration would be the very antithesis of their decorative philosophy based on subtle harmonies and gentle contrasts. Apart from these aesthetic considerations, it would also have seemed rather impractical, especially on joinery, where the surface is subjected to so much wear and tear. An English writer, advocating, in 1882, the covering of the ceiling with a 'rich cream' wallpaper, stated that 'a mere white wall overhead conveys the sorry impression that the house is left naked in every corner or spot not likely to be gazed at.'[14] Again the underlying conviction that plainness was shameful is evident.

A sense of order prevailed in Victorian decoration as it did in so many aspects of life. Contrary to the deluge of impressions of Victorian decoration that have come down to us, and that continue to be regurgitated by contemporary writers, rooms were not just a random pot-pourri of gaudy papers and heavy colours buried under bric-a-brac. Words such as florid, dramatic, theatrical, vulgar and cluttered hardly do justice to the serious attempts of the Victorians to decorate their houses harmoniously and tastefully. A lack of colour photographs of the period, a modern bias towards sterile functionalism and an ignorance of the spirit, philosophy and conventions of the age largely explain these anti-Victorian attitudes.

Far from being hedonistic, coarse and vulgar, the decoration of rooms was highly systematic and organized. Each room had a distinct aura of its own relating directly to its general purpose and chief occupants. A drawing-room, for example, was the natural vehicle for expressing feminine personality and was consequently made to appear light, pretty, informal and, above all, interesting to the visitor. Ideally, it reflected the individuality and charm of the lady of the house. The dining-room, in contrast, bore the imprint of masculine solemnity on its symmetrical contours and arrangements of furniture. Colours were more subdued and the contents chosen for their impressiveness and sobriety. The library was somewhat similar. Books, *objets d'art* and collections gave this room its special identity. Entrance halls were designed to look cool and impressive as well as welcoming. Bedrooms had a lighter airy atmosphere akin to that of the drawing-room but with a greater emphasis on comfort and softness. Other rooms such as bathrooms and kitchens did not normally warrant a highly ornamented approach and were basically practical. By the late 1880s bathrooms were beginning to be seen as worthy of extra attention. Decorative fittings and tiles were used to great effect at Mandeville Hall at Toorak and Labassa at Caulfield in Victoria, as well as in less spectacular houses.

In general, decoration was governed by strict canons of appropriateness relating to usage, style, colour, ornament and furnishing. The fact that the rules allowed considerable latitude and variety of approach in some areas did not mean that fundamental principles could be ignored.

Within the compass of those principles there was room for considerable diversity of expression. Some houses were decorated in a much more restrained mode than others, but to each was meted out a degree of ornament appropriate to the aspirations and means of its owner. Each room was endowed with a planned cohesiveness, all the elements, simple or sophisticated, being brought into harmony. No matter how modest the room, it had its own dominant theme of colour and style to give it character.

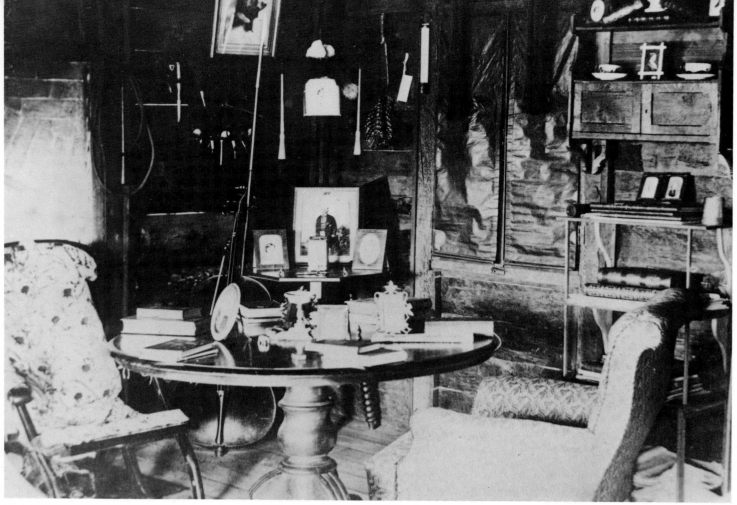

Devoid of extraneous frills, this primitive Queensland room possesses warmth and a particular charm. Its contents are neatly arranged around the unlined room, a cello rests against a corner table, a rack of pipes hangs on the walls, while an assortment of mementos, photographs, books are spread on the round table, with the rocker and easy chair near at hand.

The Australian scene was somewhat different from the English one. Despite an adherance to fundamental values and tastes, the contours of architecture and decoration were shaped by unique factors in Australia. On the one hand, the freedom to build and decorate as one saw fit was greater than in most other countries, while on the other hand, the choices of styles and materials and the aspirations were more limited. The outcome was that, in general, there tended to be less variety and experimentation, except in the province of the most wealthy, where it was practised to good effect. Average home-owners were satisfied with houses that exhibited very little individuality. Being able to conform offered especial pleasure. The absence, comparatively, of a wealthy aristocracy, the more general distribution of wealth and the distance from England all tended to promote a different set of rules.

In certain respects, Australia was free to plot its own course through the latter half of the nineteenth century, unencumbered by anxieties of direction and style. The one way to go was forward if you could manage it. A single-minded spirit of self-improvement prevailed. The stepping stones to success were before the general population, leading on beyond the wildest expectations most people could have sustained in their former homelands. To achieve the independence and stature of owning a home — any home — was the first big step, not achieved by all but enjoyed by those who were successful. The greater the subsequent steps were, the grander and more pretentious houses became. There was little trifling with variety, the joy of conformity taking precedence for the upwardly mobile society. Possibly soul-searching was not the preoccupation of architects in the nineteenth century that it was to become in the twentieth century when more basic needs had been met. Rather the purpose and path seemed clear. To build well and handsomely, to the extent that you could afford, was the goal. To decorate interiors impressively and warmly was the aim. To achieve these ends, all forces were mustered; no opportunity was passed up.

An unabashed enthusiasm and forthrightness characterizes, in the main, Australian buildings of Queen Victoria's reign. The period from 1860 to 1890 was exceptionally stable, productive, expansive and uncomplicated. No self-conscious

Rows of leaning books, a rocking chair and a kerosene lamp suggest many hours peacefully spent.

introspection marred the impetus of building or the proliferation of a general Victorian style. In Australia, more homogeneity of style characterized buildings than would have been possible if economic and geographic factors had not exerted their particular pressures.

But the favourite type of Australian house is laid out in an oblong block bisected by a three to eight foot passage. The first door on one side as you go in is the drawing-room, on the other the dining-room. Then follow the bedrooms, etc., with the kitchen and scullery at the end of the passage, or sometimes in a lean-to at right angles to the hinder part of the house proper. This kind of cottage is almost universal in Adelaide amongst the middle and upper middle classes, and invariable in the working-class throughout Australia. In the other colonies the upper middle classes often live in two-storied houses; i.e. ground-floor and one floor above.[15]

An obvious aspect of this formula for the average house was the diminution of splendour from the front to the back. The prescribed order was that the socially significant rooms warranted the most elaborate treatment while the areas devoted to functions of the family were relegated to inferior positions and treatments.

Lamenting the lack of variety of styles in decoration of the Australian upper classes in 1892, the visiting English architect, Wells, made these observations:

The ever present regret one feels in the colonies is that so little [high class work] is in demand. The country is probably too young and feels itself bound to be content with humbler things until it can afford better. Cheapness is held to be the criterion of merit and not quality. Things are different in England . . . I suppose things will improve here as we develop a richer and more leisured class. As this class grows, so the appreciation for art work of every description will grow with it. A consummation much to be desired.[16]

By the time these comments were made, architecture and decoration had already come a long way. At the time of Queen Victoria's coronation in 1838, Melbourne was but four years old, an embryonic collection of rough timber huts and a small number of two-storey brick houses. In a mere fifty years, however, it was transformed into a thriving metropolis with all the accoutrements of Victorian

Without any of the extra trimmings of wall-paper, this corner of a Queensland drawing-room, photographed about 1890, tells much of the pleasures and tastes of a modest family. A bonnet is placed casually on the chaise-longue, a work basket open on the gypsy table, waltzes on the piano, as well as the pretty vase atop a symmetrical pile of boxes, amount to a compact picture of Victorian pastimes.

civilization. Progress was rapid. Social mobility was extraordinary. A sense of pride was everywhere.

It was observed in 1883:

In the growth of towns, as well as in the progress of individuals and institutions, there are three periods to be gone through. Here the first stage is that of the log hut. This is succeeded by the weather-board cottage, which in turn gives way to brick and stucco. Finally, comes the stone building, with its two or three stories.[17]

This pattern of fairly rapid transition from the primitive to the palatial was also reflected in interiors and did much to heighten the general response to improvements in what was available to decorate homes by the 1870s. Rejoicing in the burgeoning supplies of goods and the buoyancy of the time, a writer in 1874 claimed:

The present moment is an epoch in the history of the internal decoration and furnishing of houses in Victoria. A golden shower of prosperity has descended upon the leading productive industries of the country, additions are daily made to the ranks of our wealthier residents, and never before has the creation of magnificent household interiors, as well as exteriors, proceeded at so great a rate. Throughout the country the owners of property are rivalling the 'homes of merrie England' in the size, conveniences, and grandeur of their residences, which not unfrequently resemble the mansions of English noblemen.[18]

One can readily imagine the joy of having even a conventional Victorian house of four, six or more rooms after spending a few years in the crude frugality of a log hut or tent. Imagine too, the impact of Melbourne's International Exhibition of 1880, with all its grandeur and brilliance, on the very people who less than forty years earlier were struggling to survive in a scarcely established, straggling little settlement of rudimentary buildings. The sense of wonder and pride it inspired must have been enormous.

Richard Twopeny, a snobbish English migrant whose father was archdeacon of Flinders in South Australia from 1865, found the wealthy colonist, on average, far too undiscriminating in his taste:

he has generally been brought up in too rough a school to furnish [his large house] even decently. His notion of furniture begins and ends with upholstery, and I doubt whether he ever comes to look upon this as more than things to sit on, stand on, lie on, eat off and drink off . . . [he is] amply satisfied with what an Englishman with one-tenth of his income would deem the barest necessaries.[19]

Without the softening effects of earlier building, many townships and suburbs looked extremely bald, uniform and new and a certain brashness, a *nouveau riche* awkwardness showed itself in interior decoration. The newness of furniture and all the other contents of a house was especially striking to the newcomer.

The Australian Croesus is generally very little of a snob though often his 'lady' has a taste for display. When this desire for grandeur has led them to furnish expensively, they are unable to furnish prettily, and usually feel much less comfortable in their drawing-room . . . than when their chairs and tables were made by a working carpenter or with their own hands out of a few deal boards.[20]

Surviving interiors of the period reflect much of this rather frantic scramble for material success and social acknowledgement at all levels. In almost all cases, the houses represent the improvement in material circumstances of the owner. Often the degree of improvement was an extraordinarily dramatic one—there are many variations on the rags to riches theme. Only Joseph Clarke's Mandeville Hall comes to mind as the expression of continued prosperity from an affluent beginning in life. His is the only house to survive intact, of someone born with a silver spoon in his mouth. The Rouses of Rouse Hill House at Windsor arrived with capital, to settle in the very early days of New South Wales. However, their

26

wealth was not in the class of the millionaire Clarke, whose family was connected with banking and politics as well as farming.

John Boyes, the builder of Wardlow in Parkville, Victoria, began as an ironmonger and eventually amassed a modest middle-class fortune for himself by building speculatively in Parkville. Captain Robert Gardiner, who built the fine house Mintaro near Romsey in Victoria, in 1882, began an adventurous life as a sixteen-year-old runaway sailor on a South Seas whaler. Eventually he made a fortune running cargo ships. He commemorated the progressive stages of his life, including the whaling episode, in four hand-painted panels on the ceiling of his drawing-room. Similarly, the creator of Ontario (Labassa), A. W. Robertson, made an enormous fortune in Cobb and Co. coaches and mining after emigrating to Australia from Canada. He incorporated two painted panels into the decoration of a ceiling in his splendid home. The pictures depict a sailing ship on the ocean and a small camel-train crossing the desert. The precise significance of the scenes is not known, but it is very likely that they represented times of adventure and hardship in Robertson's life before he became so successful and wealthy. Most Victorian rooms in the country were the manifestation of steadily acquired wealth, rather than the meteoric success of city merchants and entrepreneurs. The drawing-rooms of Belmont at Raglan and Navarre near Ararat, both in Victoria, reflect an improvement in the quality of life rather than the advent of sudden wealth.

Melbourne was Mecca for the merchant princes. Possessors of immense fortunes often gained in spectacular transactions, they rivalled each other in building magnificent mansions. Far from being anchored to the decorative conformity of the middle classes, they enjoyed the greatest freedom. The most spectacular flirtations with style, the most capricious enterprises in building were

Above: At Pastoria, near Kyneton, Victoria, the dining-room dado and filling paper retain their original freshness of design and beautiful colours. The dado with its upper and lower border was machine-printed in one piece. (See exterior page 16.)

Left: The Abbey, Annandale, Sydney. The sideboard in the dining-room is a rare example of the Gothic style in furniture made to complement the overall character of the house. Full of rich detailing and artwork, it indicates the high standard reached by the local firm of Lyon and Cottier, which was responsible for the decoration of the house. Tiles form the dado as well as the floor covering. Above the dado, elaborate stencilling has been painted over, but is to be restored.

Far from the conventional, this extravagant interior of Tudor Lodge shows knights in armour, heraldic shields, lofty Elizabethan spaces enriched by timber panelling.

This Queensland interior follows the popular practices in decoration of the day.

Although the twentieth century intrudes slightly into this picture, the attention to decorative detail and the ornaments, as well as the demeanour of its occupants, add greatly to its quality.

the province of the élite in the new society—these merchants, financiers and land developers. Few of their monuments to success survive, apart from the following in Victoria: J. M. Davies' mansion in Malvern (now Malvern Grammar), Kamesburgh at Brighton, Illawarra at Toorak and Labassa. However, many fascinating descriptions of these houses and their owners can be found in Michael Cannon's *Land Boomers* and *Land, Boom and Bust*. In each case the owner gave full rein to his imagination and aspirations, paying scant attention to the conventions of middle-class building styles. Excursions into Queen Anne, Norman, Tudor and Renaissance styles were part of the varied outcome of their architectural enterprise and wealth.

It is in this context that the interiors of Illawarra, Labassa and Mandeville Hall should be considered. Eager to display their fortunes and flamboyance, the owners embarked on stylistic adventures of fantastic splendour. Each sought to invest his house with that little bit extra, a stylistic novelty for all to admire. Clarke's Mandeville Hall captured the artistic quality of the English Aesthetic movement for his main rooms and capped it with the exoticism of an Indian room.

Just before the economic bubble burst in 1892, the architect James Birtwistle built Illawarra for C. H. James: a house of Queen Anne proportions commanding a splendid view from its lofty tower. It is owned by the National Trust of Australia (Victoria) and is structurally though not decoratively intact. The interior is robust and colourful, the main techniques of decoration being painted and stencilled work. Solid massive joinery adds to the strong character of the interior.

Naturally, some differences emerged in the development of architecture and decoration from city to city. Sydney and Hobart, with their bulwark of early buildings, were not nearly as much transformed by the rush of Victorian buildings that shaped the face of Melbourne and Adelaide. Perhaps those pre-Victorian buildings had a steadying effect not felt by the citizens in the younger cities. The stock of older buildings would have cushioned the effect of rapid growth. It was said:

in Melbourne houses are certainly more expensively, and perhaps better furnished than in any of the other towns. The Victorians have a much greater love of show than any of their fellow-Australians. Where a Sydney man spends £400 on his furniture you may safely predict that a Melbourner will spend £600.[21]

Dotted across the countryside from Maitland in New South Wales to Ross in Tasmania were mansions emulating the English country house. Some sought to create a miniature world of the English gentry complete with fox hunts and deer-stalking. The climax in the history of such houses probably was the Duke of Edinburgh's visit in 1868. He stayed at various important houses including the Austins' Barwon Park at Winchelsea, Victoria. The balls, festivities and sporting events would no doubt have given the owners great satisfaction. To entertain royalty would have filled to overflowing the cups of the successful.

In their design and decoration, most of these houses clung closely to the typical English prototype, never straying far from the grandiose and the ponderous. They had large entrance halls, often grand staircases, splendid big rooms for entertaining and a substantial wing for servants. Werribee Park at Werribee in Victoria is one such survivor. Having recently undergone some painstaking restoration and reconstruction, it is now an interesting and complete house of the grandest scale.

One may well ask where, in the distant antipodes, did the decorative material come from? The answer is that on the whole, it was imported from England. Nevertheless, many local industries grew up catering for building and decorating needs. By the 1880s there were cast-iron foundries, plasterworks, wallpaper manufacturers and furniture-makers but still many products were imported.

Encaustic tiles for verandahs and entrance halls, ceramic tiles, slates, marble, light-fittings, linoleums, carpets and wallpapers as well as furniture were imported on a tremendous scale. The upper end of the market remained firmly attached to England as a source of most items of decoration. Some items, including fabrics for furnishing, were made in France, and came to Australia by way of London. Paintings and other ornaments came from various parts of Europe, especially Italy.

Periodic pilgrimages of the wealthy to London yielded masses of the most fashionable household goods. Generally though, the householder put her faith in the styles presented by the local importers, and thereby helped to perpetuate certain styles here, even when they had been superseded in England. The local merchant was understandably only interested in promoting items of known commercial viability, not in improving taste or advancing new theories of decoration. One of these firms of successful importers was W. H. Rocke and Company of Melbourne. They had a thriving business. Among other examples, they are known to have supplied the furniture to the council chamber of Fitzroy Town Hall. In order to promote their goods, in 1874 they published a little booklet called *Remarks on House Furnishing and House Decoration*. It gives a very good insight into the contemporary style of furnishing and the range of goods. Alluding to the significant role of importers it states:

One could not better demonstrate the real advancement made by Victoria during late years than by pointing to the mighty difference between the drawing-rooms of our 'upper ten' a dozen years ago, and what they are now. It implies a social revolution in which we, as furnishers, are proud to have had a hand.[22]

Not everyone rejoiced in the influence of importers and local manufacturers on furnishing. They were seen by some, Rocke for example, to be largely responsible for the 'entire want of individuality about the Australian's house.' Twopeny found it surprising that the average Australian's individuality, which was so pronounced in his career and his personality, was so far from expressing itself in his choice of furnishing. He commented:

The furniture imported or (in Melbourne) made by the large upholsterers is, with few exceptions, more gorgeous than pretty; whence one may reasonably infer that the taste of their customers—when they have any—is better suited by the grandiose than the artistic. But most of the expensively furnished houses show plainly that the upholsterer has been given carte blanche *to do what he will. Look at his shop-window and you may make a shrewd guess at his customer's drawing-room.*[23]

From the late 1880s a marked extremism of design developed. Decoration became more profuse, not to say excessive. Dados crept high up the wall; cornices fairly dripping with ornament came down towards them. Ceiling roses stretched weighty tentacles across the ceiling. The elements of decoration, both internally and externally, became heavy and unmanageable. Victorian decoration could go no further—to proceed would be to regress. The limits of the philosophy of ornament had finally been reached. A sense of exhaustion with it all engulfed the decorators and perhaps the householders, heralding the need for a fresh force and a new approach.

The disastrous financial crash of the 1890s punctured optimism completely. All but a few were scathed and sobered by the experience. When decoration emerged from the ashes of the Victorian period it was with chastened humility. The zest and zoom of the 1880s were left behind and in their place were the sensible qualities of simplicity and moderation. Rich wallpapers and polychromatic decoration were expelled and their place taken by open, milder forms of decoration. With more hesitant steps, Australian decoration moved towards an expression of national sentiment combining an adaptation of Queen Anne revival architecture and Art Nouveau embellishment.

Packed with furnishing of the period, this late Victorian showroom gives many clues to the fashionable designs and styles of upholstery.

A splendid display by W. H. Rocke of upholstered luxury and curvaceous styling in drawing-room furniture in 1874.

The showroom of W. H. Rocke again shows us 'a fair sample of modern taste in one direction', with little that is 'genuine old English' and much that is impressive.

CHAPTER ONE

The Drawing-Room

From many points of view the drawing-room is the most important room in the house, and it generally is one on which the individuality of the womenkind is most markedly impressed. It is an important room, if for no other reason than that it is the link between the outside world and the inhabitants of the house—the neutral ground where callers can penetrate without further approach to intimacy, and from that stand-point gather their impressions of what lies beyond—of what are the tastes, intellectual pursuits and characteristics of the occupiers of the home.[1]

The drawing-room at Bedervale, near Braidwood in New South Wales uses the pastel shades often chosen for drawing-rooms. Curiously, the main paper was produced in the 1850s and the dado was made closer to 1880, suggesting that the latter was added when the fashion for dados was irresistible in the 1880s.

SURELY NO OTHER ROOM IN THE VICTORIAN HOUSE has excited such extreme reactions as the drawing-room. Eulogized in its time as the pride of every woman's home and the high point of artistic expression, it became the target of savage criticism in the twentieth century. On the one hand frilly, sentimental images have cloyed its reputation while on the other, scathing remarks have attacked its falseness and sickliness.

The Victorian drawing-room, created with a new kind of bourgeois zeal and pride, gave their mistresses a domain of amazing autonomy. A great deal of thought and effort went into making the room a successful talking-point as well as a source of social prestige. Generally, the decoration, furnishings and small items were selected by the lady of the house, often in conjunction with 'a fashionable decorator and upholsterer'.[2]

In retrospect, the drawing-room was perceived as the epitome of Victorian life. All that was thought to be superficial and hypocritical about Victorian society was associated with the drawing-room, regarded by some as an absurd cocoon of femininity in an otherwise male-dominated society. The extent to which Victorian drawing-rooms were misrepresented, misunderstood and under-rated will be explored through these pages.

It is apparent that the sheer individuality, the stylistic assertiveness of the drawing-room, caused it to be ridiculed, if not caricatured. In England in the 1870s and in Australia in the 1880s articles were written that made a mockery of Victorian decoration and drawing-rooms in particular.

[They] pick out the enrichments of ceiling and cornice with all the colours of the rainbow, cover the floor with a carpet whereupon the whole contents of a conservatory have been upset . . . purchase a round centre table whose legs bristle with leaves and flowers and twining snakes, all glued together in one shapeless mass and the chairs, en suite . . . their brilliance preserved from tarnish by crocheted antimacassars. The sofa is designed with a strict disregard of comfort and convenience: its head is turned one way and its legs are turned another, the construction being quite concealed by lumpy padding; but here and there, whenever it is most in the way, appears an acanthus leaf, a boss or a claw, all convulsed with a desire to be sufficiently elegant for a drawing-room.[3]

Filmy drapes and wispy floral
arrangements give this New South
Wales interior an ethereal quality.
Note the branched gaselier with counter
balancers to adjust height.

Rooms such as this were no doubt
responsible for the poor reputation
Victorian interiors have acquired!
They became easy prey to charges of
overcrowding and excessive clutter. For
all that, they are filled with interest
and historic data. Note, among other
things, the decorated door panels.

The intense pleasure the rooms gave their owners and the almost wholesale conversion of society to the mid-Victorian decorative style thoroughly irked those who saw in it nothing but 'the signs of ugliness'—and foolishness.[4] The fact that it was a popular, visually oriented style, not inspired, nurtured or restrained by intellectual considerations, tormented the critics. Technical ingenuity and highly mechanized workmanship were not qualities to be readily appreciated at close range. In fact it is only after a century has elapsed and anti-Victorian opinion has died down that the achievement and artistry of Victorian decoration can be fairly assessed.

The drawing-room underwent some significant stylistic changes during Queen Victoria's long reign. There was a marked transition from early to middle Victorian style around 1850 and again from middle to late style in the 1890s, though the first rumblings of the latter could be heard much earlier in England. Broadly, early Victorian drawing-room design was rather formal, restrained and classical with a distinctive undercurrent of the Regency style. Though colours were very rich, the full impact of mass-produced wallpapers and furniture had not been felt. By about the middle of the century, perhaps a decade later in Australia, restraint gave way to an expansive and bold phase that culminated in the 1880s building boom. During the feverish burst of building activity, drawing-rooms were decorated with unparalleled optimism, spiritedness and abundance of sumptuous contents that characterized the boom period.

A reaction against this hedonistic episode set in as early as the 1870s in England but did not greatly alter the direction of style until much later. The 1870s and 1880s saw the emergence of many new styles. English leaders in design such as Morris, Talbert, Eastlake, Day and Dresser each, in his own way, urged a change from the eclectic combinations of the drawing-room to a style more distinctive and more artistic. Mandeville Hall is an interesting example of *avant-garde* decoration reflecting the English influences. By the general standards of taste current at the time in Australia, the decoration of Mandeville Hall in 1876 was a decade ahead of its contemporaries, being more in line with the embryonic Arts and Crafts movement in England.

In Australia, the mid-Victorian mood remained largely unshattered until the early 1890s when the change coincided with an economic depression. Consequently, mid-Victorian drawing-rooms in Australia had a curious uniformity of style that was commented upon by visitors. Twopeny wrote with exasperation in 1883:

The frowsy carpets and heavy solid chairs of England's cold and foggy climate reign supreme beneath the Austral sun. The Exhibitions have done something towards reforming our domestic interiors, but it will be a long time before the renaissance of art as applied to households, which appears to be taking place in England, makes its way here in any considerable force.[5]

Despite the distinctiveness of the first and last phases of the era, the mid-Victorian style predominates. Victoria and South Australia especially have a magnificent building stock of mid-Victorian houses and public buildings. A small number of buildings with their drawing-rooms still intact decoratively can be found in most parts of Australia. The giants of those surviving are Meningoort at Terang, Labassa, Mintaro and Werribee Park (Victoria), Mona Vale near Ross and Woolmers near Launceston (Tasmania), and The Acacias at Marryatville and Yallum Park at Penola (South Australia). In the ranks of the more modest are the drawing-rooms of Merigal at Nowra and Rouse Hill House (New South Wales), Ralahyne at Brisbane (Queensland), and Ceres near Ballarat, Mynda at Kew, Westella at Hawthorn, Belmont, Navarre and Wardlow (Victoria).

Examples from the earlier period in Tasmania and New South Wales are now extremely rare. In Sydney, Elizabeth Bay House, begun in 1835, is a fine example of an early Victorian building that has been restored to display the decoration and furnishings of that period. On a more modest scale, Georgiana McCrae's homestead, built in isolation on the shores of Port Phillip Bay, Victoria, in 1847, is an example of a restored interior with an early Victorian character, and the furnishings in particular are largely original. In Tasmania, Summerhome near Hobart has much of its early Victorian decoration intact. Otherwise the evidence of early Victorian decoration is generally fragmented; we can see a scrap of wallpaper here, a piece of furniture there, but a glimpse of the drawing-room in its entirety is denied us.

As the number of houses being built virtually came to a standstill in the 1890s, there are relatively few examples of houses constructed in the late-Victorian phase and few of these are still intact decoratively. Pastoria near Kyneton in Victoria is one such example, the renovation of which is dated 1894. Architecturally, it presents some interesting innovations. The drawing-room, however, is decorated on fairly conventional lines with naturalistic floral wallpapers, ornate ceiling roses and cornices and oak wood-graining. Just a little adventure in the design of the windows, with coloured glass panels in the upper third, and full length french doors opening on to the garden, gives a hint of change.

When building finally resumed after the depression it was in a new style heavily indebted to the Queen Anne style which was much later described as Federation. In drawing-rooms a plainer, more controlled effect was aimed at, with more open space, less decoration and sparser furnishing. Glenhope, built in 1895 in Pennant Hills, outer Sydney, is an interesting example of this later period. The walls are hung with an off-white ground, floral wallpaper with matching frieze while the ceiling is simply off-white. The key architectural elements are the inglenook fireplace and the circular corner window with its simpler fretwork decoration.

Returning to the mid-Victorian drawing-room, we should now look at its qualities in detail. What was the average middle-class drawing-room like in the 1880s? How was it conceived by its creators and how was it decorated and furnished?

Some contemporary descriptions of drawing-rooms survive. Mostly very personal, they provide an interesting insight into decoration. The most rhapsodic

Stencil designs for the decoration of a drawing-room. Fig. 1—Dado above skirting in borders and panels. Fig. 2—Frieze below cornice. Figs 3 and 4—Designs for borders. Fig. 5—Treatment of lower (A) and upper (B) panels of door and ornamental work above door.

Left: Wallpapers, paint colours and most of the furnishings have survived the ravages of time and fashion in Belmont's modest drawing-room, which was added to the older homestead in 1888. The ceiling is plain painted pine, the cornice a simple timber band and the frieze accordingly modest.

Above: The drawing-room at Glenhope, Sydney, gives a glimpse of the new fashions of the late Victorian drawing-room. Timber fretwork makes its appearance, glazing patterns have changed and, most noticeably, white has emerged as a decorative colour. Ceiling and cornice are tinted with pink. The filling paper and frieze, softly merged, have altered in relation to the picture rail, which has dropped in height significantly. A strong contrast is built up between dark stained joinery and pastel tones.

A Victorian drama unfolds against a background of wallpaper decoration and a fancy door.

was that of the local furnisher and upholsterer, Rocke, who in 1874 wrote a booklet of remarks on decoration for the middle-class housewife. It is liberally sprinkled with sales promotions but nevertheless provides an excellent source of information, on furnishing especially. He gives a full list of all possible items one could wish for in an upper middle-class drawing-room. He also voices the fundamental attitudes people held towards their drawing-rooms:

That one room in every house suggests ideas of poetry and beauty, as well as of comfort and decency, is a vast national blessing. It must tend to exalt and enrich the mind. And when wealth is at hand to heighten the ornamental effect, the case is all the stronger. Such apartments are a fair field for aesthetic gratification and artistic luxury.[6]

The drawing-room was the province of the artistic, the refined and the aesthetic, quite untarnished by utilitarianism. As such its decoration was soft, elegant and harmonious. The colours favoured were French grey, cream, gold and blue with sometimes a dash of rose pink. In style, the decorations and furnishings were inspired by French fashions, curves and cabrioles abounding by the 1880s. Lightness of form and colour of furniture was emphasized, the most popular wood being walnut. Gilding of special parts, cornices, ceiling roses, frames, furniture and ornaments followed naturally for a room where everything was chosen for its contribution to an effect of beauty and richness.

Some drawing-rooms were hung with wallpapers combining a main wall design with a coordinated frieze. Elegant French motifs were favoured as well as the flowing lines of flowers, birds and other designs from nature. The friezes occupied the most eye-catching space below the cornice and were often very stylish with garlands, scrolls, medallions, birds and other spectacular elements. Frequently the ceiling, which warranted considerable attention, was elaborately stencilled but often a symmetrical or silvery 'star' motif wallpaper would be used instead. Stencilling could also decorate the walls though this was more usual in hallways and other rooms. In general, the more modest middle-class houses such as Belmont used wallpapers, and those on a slightly grander scale used painted surfaces and elaborate stencilling such as that at Mintaro. Simple stencilling was found in a variety of situations, including the front rooms of terrace houses and cottages. Whatever the material or technique, the effect sought was delicate and subtle, as well as rich and impressive.

A number of smaller, colourful decorative items—cushions, pictures, ornaments, flowers and general bric-a-brac—contributed to the harmonious blend of soft colours and patterns in the drawing-room. Bracket gaseliers, usually brass with tinted shades, were used to light the room, as well as a central gaselier.

Since chairs were not placed against the wall, but were rather casually arranged in clusters about the room, the dado was not considered necessary and was therefore often omitted from the decorative scheme.

The prescribed white marble chimneypiece was crowned by an elegant and large gilded overmantel mirror, and the mantelpiece arrayed with a central gilded 'pendule' (clock) flanked by pairs of vases (some of them quite enormous), lustres, and statuettes, all delicately ornamented.

A handsome piano, perhaps walnut, occupied a key space in the room, perhaps by the window. Ornaments, vases, statues, photographs and anything else would be arranged on its draped top. A touch of the exotic—a Japanese fan or a stuffed bird of paradise or somesuch—added greatly to the vitality of the room.

A display cabinet, a work table, a suite of shapely chairs comprising lady's and gentleman's chairs, sofa and half-a-dozen single chairs and various small tables would rest their fine feet on a pastel-toned swirly, floral bordered carpet, probably a 'Brussels'.

Sumptuous drapes of silk, damask or cretonne and window curtains of lace, probably Nottingham, augmented the delicacy and repose of the room. Scattered palms and ferns in jardinieres provided the final garnishing.

The merchant Rocke uses a particular large summer drawing-room—'a light and airy apartment'—as a model for his customers. His description provides a wealth of detail and insight:

The door is at one end; on the right is a projecting fireplace of the purest white marble; on the left, two windows, each in a slight embrasure; and at the end is a curtained portal leading into a conservatory. Through the looped curtains may be seen a pyramidal group of greenery surrounded by flower-pots and flanked by gracefully moulded jardinieres. Other jardinieres singly occupy each window embrasure. Once the walls were hung with fluted silk, of a French grey tint, but now they are simply painted that colour and relieved by oblong panels of gold beading, which is also carried along the line where the walls and ceiling meet . . . A few intertwined sprays of delicate Australian blossoms, hand-painted, form the central ornament of each panel. No gasalier hangs from the ceiling, but there are elegant gilt bracket lamps on each side of the room, and candelabra, simulating, according to Parisian fashion, the form of wax candles, with dependent lustres, help to equalise the artificial light afforded. Ground glass shades tone down the glare. The next striking feature of the room is the carpet [which is a 'Brussels']. The chosen pattern is as new as it is striking and picturesque. Its prevailing colour is French grey blended with oak, and minute touches of blue. The design consists of floriated tracery, relieved by small arabesques in oak on a black ground. The coverings of the furniture are of cretonne—the admirable cotton cloth that has cast almost all the ordinary chintzes into the cold shades of unfashionableness. Its pattern, purely French, consists of arabesques, varied by medallions and vases alternately, in black and gold, on a ground tinged with a salmon shade of pink. The curtains are of the same material. Those over the conservatory entrance are looped to hang low, have no bordering, but are trimmed with silk cord, and lining them are an inner pair of Nottingham lace curtains, the whole surmounted by cretonne hangings trimmed with Paris silk fringe. On the contrary, the window curtains come from under handsome gilt cornices. A few small water-colour drawings and photographs are allowed to appear at intervals on the walls, but they do not add much to the general effect. On the mantelpiece are statuettes in alabaster and porcelain, Bohemian vases of a kind the most pure and chic ever seen in the colony, and a tall mirror six feet high by four feet wide, in a carved wooden (not composition) frame, richly gilt and strictly angular. The crowning ornament is a medallion supported by open work. There is no fender and the Angora hearthrug is drawn close to the fireplace. We turn next to examine the articles of furniture in the room . . . Here are two console tables, slabs of marble supported by gilt cabriole legs, and surmounted by tall mirrors reaching to the ceiling. No centre table is to be seen, but its place is occupied by a three-seated centre ottoman, framed in carved walnut, and corresponding with an S-shaped conversation chair. The sofa is real French in shape, and it is decorated by light carvings in walnut, that suggest simplicity as well as ornateness. The fauteuils (for lady and gentleman) are circular-seated, with stuffed backs framed in walnut, which are narrow at the bottom, but spread out upwards almost like a fan. In this instance, as in other pieces of comparatively heavy stuffed furniture, the cretonne is trimmed at the edges with fancy gilt nails, each headed like a fleur-de-lis. The other easy chairs are of the American folding pattern, and now known by their quaint appelation of 'kangaroo' chairs. Attention is next attracted to the gilded furniture; the brilliant sumptuousness of which seems to illuminate the whole room. Here is a gilt ottoman, shaped like the mediaeval Glastonbury chair, the curved outlines of its supports enriched by little tricks of crossbar ornament. It is more or less matched in style, as well as colour, by a music-stool of light framework, a few ordinary drawing-room chairs with ornamental open-work at back, and a prie-dieu, *or devotional chair, supported by carved feet, and having for the central ornament of its back a long Latin cross. The eye, having rested so long on the more obvious details of the room, now turns to its more precious contents. Nothing can be finer in their way than the two cabinets which stand against the wall, and are surmounted by busts and a few precious morsels of antique art. They are choice specimens of the reigning favourite pattern in Paris, where fashion (eagerly followed in England) has adopted ebony as a ground colour, to be set off with inlaid arabesques and lines of choice ormolu. One cabinet is of black and gold, with lines of inlaid walnut to relieve the top and sides. A thick glass door discloses the interior, lined with rose velvet. The other displays less gold, its chief beauty being its zebra-*

FIREPLACE

CONSERVATORY

WALLS

LIGHTS

CARPET

FURNITURE
COVERINGS

CURTAINS

PICTURES
ORNAMENTS

MIRROR

FURNITURE

An interior, c. 1880, shows that walls were not always elaborately decorated with wallpaper, stencilling or deep shades of paintwork. In some houses pastel shades were used, or even very rarely, plain plaster with extra colour in the cornice. The drapes on the chandelier, chimneypiece and windows are also interesting.

Above: By alternating three shades of brown and two of blue, the cornice successfully captures the superb colour combination of the wallpaper in the drawing-room of Navarre Station, Victoria.

Right: Dispensing with the usual dado and frieze, this late Victorian drawing-room in a modest single-fronted cottage in North Melbourne is nevertheless full of Victorian charm. The wallpaper is complemented by the tinted cornice and wood-grained joinery.

wood inlayings. Our space permits no further description of these superb pieces of furniture, any more than of the costly cheffonnier sideboard of walnut, mirror-backed, whose carvings and inlayings of arabesques in white sycamore are in a style of art hitherto almost unknown to Australia. Adjoining the piano, a fine Parisian Erard, is a canterbury of black and gold, resembling the cabinets, and on its slab top an alabaster vase of flowers under a glass shade. The ormolu is beaded, and its richness is enhanced by inlayings of sycamore stained green. Within the plateglass door are compartments for song, dance, sacred, and general music. On the far side of the room, near the window, is a davenport of ebony black relieved by panels of musk, in the centre of which are antique cameos in porcelain. The interior is fitted with white sycamore and satinwood, and on each side are nests of drawers. Disposed in different parts of the room are two of those little Japanese (of French workmanship, however) receptacles for ladies' work, supported on light bamboo folding frames, that no modern drawing-room ought to be without. Elsewhere is a more massive ladies' work-table, of walnut, sumptuously carved and inlaid; its top is double, and, when opened and turned half round, is found inlaid for the purposes of chess, backgammon, and cribbage. To match are 'occasional' tables in the same style, and on opening them they supply all the requisites of a card-table. The only other tables in the room are two or three of those small round-topped tripod sort, known variously as 'monkey' and 'gipsy' tables, which have of late come into extensive demand, not only for ordinary drawing-room purposes, but also for those of the new-fashioned 'five o'clock tea'. The legs are knotted and gilt, and the top is covered with a cloth bordered by a deep fringe that hangs over the edge. The means of comfort and convenience are supplemented by footstools, some like miniature camp-stools, the framework gilt and the web quilted silk; other, of white

enamel and gold, circular, covered with Berlin wool work; other carved, and others of ebony and gold. Such are the leading features of this beautiful drawing-room . . .[7]

Mr Rocke offers another variation on the theme with his description of the winter drawing-room.

The winter drawing-room of this house does not call for such minute description, because its main difference from the other lies in the prevailing colour employed. Thus, the coverings of the furniture are of rich crimson satin which matches the deep neutral tint of the painted walls, which are bordered close to the ceiling with a Pompeiian pattern in black and red. In the carpet, variously shaped panels with a black ground are relieved by flowers in blue and red. The articles of furniture are in the main the same, only differently disposed, as in the summer room, save that the occasional chairs are fewer, their place being taken by ordinary drawing-room chairs en suite. *Instead of a conservatory entrance, there is an embayed window, under which is a settee stuffed to match the chairs. Above is a gilt cornice, from which depend on each side silk rep curtains, coming from under straight silk drapery with a cut border trimmed with Paris fringe. Behind these are lace curtains, one pair to each of the three compartments of the window, looped not by hangers, but by white gimp bands. Further, the fireplace has a fender of polished steel and ormolu, and the fire-irons are silvered. Fronting it are gilt fire-screens and a fender-stool of ebony varied by lines of gold work and standing on gilt eagles' feet grasping a black ball.*[8]

His description of both drawing-rooms leaves little to the imagination and

Woolmers in Tasmania offers a rare opportunity to view a grand early Victorian drawing-room. Especially choice are the deep rose drapes, complete with tassels. Scattered about the room, on the original body and border carpet, are pieces of the large rosewood suite. The room is thought to have been decorated in preparation for the visit of the Duke of Edinburgh in 1868 and re-papered sometime this century.

Sir William Shields and his children at Summerland House, St Kilda, Victoria. Note the plethora of floral arrangements, the vivid floral carpet and the draped chimneypiece.

An air of ease and comfort surrounds Sir William Knox's late Victorian drawing-room at Ranfurlie, East Malvern, Victoria.

almost nothing to chance. It amounts to a catalogue of contents for home-owners. He has a few extra words to say about the Gothic style that was becoming popular in Australia, albeit a little slowly.

A word about those Gothic designs for drawing-room furniture which are so highly popular in certain somewhat limited circles. Modern art has done wonders in imparting to an ordinary drawing-room, as well as dining-room, and even bedroom fittings and decorations that quaint mediaeval aspect, which, albeit consistent with the utmost elaboration of ornament, is frequently marked by a tone more or less ecclesiastical. The great beauty and impressiveness of the Gothic style are fully displayed in our Show-rooms, but we have in the main employed it more for dining-rooms, libraries, and halls, than drawing-rooms.[9]

Other writers tackled the same kind of conventional drawing-rooms but without Rocke's enthusiasm. Blistering attacks on the *nouveau riche* quality of Australian society laced some accounts. Twopeny looked at Australia from a strictly English point of view and a snobbish one at that. Seldom were his sympathies aroused for the inhabitants, who were struggling to create civilized and comfortable surroundings for themselves. He complained that 'the inevitable "newness" of everything cannot but strike the eye disagreeably . . . the style of your house becomes a mere matter of pounds, shillings and pence.'[10] From the aloofness of his upper-class English background he poured scorn on the machinations of local society and the often awkward attempts to decorate houses. With the invention of his typical upper middle-class character he named Muttonwool, and other representational identities, he gives a lively account of decorative trends. He finds little to admire in general but he admits 'there are a little number of people in Australia, and especially in Victoria, who have as good an idea of how to furnish as other middle-class Englishmen — though perhaps that is not saying much.'[11]

A spicy satirical flavour pervades Twopeny's description of houses, ranging from those of the most wealthy through the various levels of the middle class, to the working class. In particular, he expresses to perfection the stratification of decoration — each level descending through society following the same furnishing formula but with less luxurious ingredients. He incisively analyses the factors separating one strata from the next and adroitly matches each level with their mode of decoration.

. . . it is time we should go through Muttonwool's house room by room. On entering the drawing-room the first thing that strikes the eye is the carpet, with a stiff set pattern large enough to knock you down, and of a rich gaudy colour. You raise your eyes—find opposite them the regulation white marble mantelpiece, more or less carved, and a gilt mirror, which we will hope is not protected from the flies by green netting. Having made a grimace, you sit down upon one of the chairs. There are nine in the room besides the sofa—perhaps an ottoman—and you can take your choice between the 'gent's' armchair, the lady's low-chair, and the six high ones. If they are not in their night-shirts you can examine the covering—usually satin or perhaps cretonne. The pattern is unique, being, I should think, specially manufactured for the colonial market. Bright hues prevail. Occasional chairs have only lately been introduced, and the whole suite is in unison, though harmony with the carpet has been overlooked, or rather never thought of, the two things having been chosen separately, and without any idea that it would be an improvement if they were to match.

As for the make of the chairs, they are to be found in plenty of English middle-class drawing-rooms even now. The shape may be named the 'deformed'. The back is carved out into various contortions of a horse-shoe, with a bar across the middle which just catches you in the small of the back, and is a continual reproach if you venture to lean against it. The wood of which the chairs are made is mahogany, walnut, or cedar. The large round or oval table which stands in the middle of the room is of the same wood, and so are the card-table, the Davenport, the chiffonier, and that Jacob's-ladder-like what-not in the corner. In some houses the upholsterer has stuffed the room with useless tables. Of course there is a fender and fire-irons, and probably a black doleful-looking grate, which during two-thirds of the year is stuffed with paper shavings of all the colours of the rainbow and several others which good Mother Nature forgot to put into it. On the chimney-piece is a Louis XVI clock and pair of ornaments to match. A piano, tune immaterial, is a sine qua non *even in a middle-class house, but when Muttonwool has got all these things—in short, paid his upholsterer's bill—he thinks a ten-pound note should cover the rest of his drawing-room furniture. Household goods are terribly deficient, and it would not be difficult to fancy yourself in a lodging-house. There may be a few odds and ends picked up on the overland route, and a set of stereotyped ornaments bought at an auction sale or sent out as 'sundries' in a general cargo; but of bric-à-brac, in the usual acceptation of the term, there is little or none.*

As for the pictures, they are altogether abominable. Can you imagine a man with £5,000 a year (or £500, for that matter) covering his walls with chromos? The inferior kinds of these 'popularizers of art,' as the papers call them, have an immense sale here. Even when a wealthy man has been told that it is his duty to buy pictures, the chances are that he will attend an auction and pick up rubbish at low prices, rubbing his hands over what he considers a good bargain; or if he wants to tell his visitors how much he gave for his pictures he gets mediocre work with a name on it. A few men have good pictures, but I hardly know anyone who has any good engravings. Muttonwool can see no difference between a proof before letters and the illustrations from the newspapers, which may be seen pasted on the walls of every small shop and working-man's cottage.

Let us now hie us to humbler abodes, and visit an eight-roomed cottage, inhabited by a young solicitor whose income is from £500 to £1000 a year. Here the whole drawing-room suite is in cretonne or rep, and comprises the couch, six chairs, and lady's and gent's easy-chairs, which we saw before at Muttonwool's. The carpet is also ditto. The glass, ornaments, etc., are similar, but on a smaller scale; and if there are any pictures on the wall they are almost bound to be chromos, for whilst Croesus sometimes invests in expensive paintings, the middle-class, who cannot afford to give from £100 upwards for a picture, will make no effort to obtain something moderately good, such as can be easily obtained in England for a very small outlay. The gasalier is bronze instead of glass.

Having seen the £600 a year cottage, it is almost needless to visit the £300 and £400, belonging to clerks and the smaller shopkeepers. The style is the same, but the quantity and quality inferior. For instance, the drawing-room carpet is tapestry instead of Brussels; the dining-room furniture is covered with horse-hair instead of leather, and so on. We will go into the next cottage—less pretentious-looking and a little smaller. The rent is twelve shillings a week, and it belongs to a carpenter in good employ. Here there is no drawing-room, but the

CARPET

MANTELPIECE

CHAIRS

TABLES

FIREPLACE

CLOCK

PIANO

BRIC-A-BRAC

PICTURES

41

The cool simplicity of the early Victorian drawing-room is captured in Henry Hopkins' retreat, Summerhome, near Hobart, Tasmania. The soft grey wallpaper simulates buttoned silk with shading around the diamond forms of the design.

parlour aspires to comfort quite undreamt of by an English tradesman. Our old friends the horsehair cedar couch, the gent's and lady's chairs together with four balloon high chairs, turn up again. There is a four-foot chiffonier, a tapestry carpet, a gilt chimney-glass, a hearthrug, a bronze fender and fire-irons, and a round table with turned pillar and carved claws.[12]

All Twopeny's characters, from wealthy Muttonwool down to poor Hornyhand, have an apparently total commitment to the direct method of buying household goods. Everything is new, owes its creation largely to mechanized processes and conforms to the prevailing dictates of fashion.

On the other hand, at the higher levels of Victorian society there was a remarkable expansion of ideas and styles in decoration. Individuality was greatly admired and the wealthy extended themselves considerably in pursuit of originality and excellence. Drawing-rooms were designed with the loftiest ideals in mind. An amazing amount of thought went into the smallest detail, while workmanship was of an extremely high standard. The drawing-rooms of Mandeville Hall and Labassa show this clearly.

In 1883, Terry and Oakden, a Melbourne based architectural firm with a high reputation, published a fine booklet in which they set out their ideas on architecture and decoration. Using English examples, they give a clear idea of the qualities of an ideal upper-class drawing-room:

The drawing-room at Grove Lodge is adorned on the theory that its function is one which requires a degree of richness bordering on brilliancy, which were out of place in a study, or studio, or a sittingroom. Here are to be happy assemblies of light-hearted people in gay dresses, and the room must be in harmony with the purpose of pleasure which has brought them together; but then the drawing-room must not obtrude itself, it must not outshine their lustres nor pale their colours; rather it must supply the company with an appropriate framing, and set them all in the best light. I have rarely seen a more picturesque drawing-room than that at Grove Lodge, and none that has seemed to me a more purely artistic creation of a beautiful out of a rather unpromisingly constructed room. A paper of heraldic pink roses, very faint, with WALLPAPER
leaves in mottled gold, makes a frieze of one width above a wall-paper of sage-grey, which has no discernible figures at all on it. This sage-gray supplies an excellent background to the pictures—which are moderate in quantity, charming in quality—and for the picturesque ladies, who are too often fairly blanched by the upholsterers' splendour, as they might be by blue and silver lights in a theatre. At the cornice is a gold moulding and fretting, making an CORNICE
agreeable fringe to the canopy (as the star-spotted ceiling may be appropriately called). The CEILING
ceiling is not stellated, however, with the regularity of wall-paper designs, but with stars of various magnitude and interspaces. It must be, of course, a room in which the deep tones of colour preponderate which could alone make such a ceiling appropriate. In this instance it is COLOUR
rendered appropriate not only by the character of the hangings of the room, at once rich and WALL-
subdued, and by the carpet, which Mr Boughton has had made for this room, the basis of whose HANGINGS
design is the green sward, touched here and there with spots of red, but also by the fact that it is a double drawing-room, lighted in the daytime only at the ends, and requiring therefore a bright ceiling.[13]

In 1892 a visiting architect, Wells, proposed a decorative approach that was gently suggestive of a new style. He espoused the use of painted areas, rather than wallpapers, while advocating rich colours and a fullness of decoration. His comments on the drawing-room can be taken as a guideline for decoration of the 1890s, for upper middle-class houses especially:

The drawing-room is the ladies' special room, and should be bright and cheerful . . . Instead of the sombre hues suited to the dining-room, soft, quiet and light effects are best, say cream or soft duck-egg shell blue or French grey for ceilings, the walls fawn colour or a richer French grey, or a deeper grey blue; approaching peacock shade, all these are good for showing ladies' complexions and dress to the best advantage, and that is a consideration not to be overlooked. Water colour drawings will also look well on these grounds, the wood-work may be creamy-white, finished with enamel varnish this gives a beautiful smooth and fresh effect. I think the judicious application of gilding in this room very advantageous, but the same remark applies to all public rooms and hall. I think it is better to gild the small enrichments of cornices solid, than to break up the ornament of the large enrichments with points of gold, what is technically called hatching or picking out. The round, the concave and small ogee mouldings always look well gilded, as their rounded surfaces catch the light from all points. The walls should be decorated with water colour drawings, or etchings tastefully arranged, choice pieces of ornamental and Doulton pottery are beautiful and very decorative. . . . I think there should be many books in the drawing-room, it is the general sitting-room and no one need ever be weary or suffer ennui, who loves good books.[14]

Notice the subtle shift the drawing-room has made from its mid-Victorian exclusivity to its becoming the general sitting-room. The notion of relaxing there and browsing through a book seems to change the emphasis on the carefully ordered pursuits associated with the room in the previous decade. The other noticeable decorative development is in the choice of creamy-white for the joinery. It heralds the fashion for light colours, pastels and cream in particular.

Almost simultaneously, in 1890 the *Sydney Illustrated News* published a series called 'Art in the Home', subtitled 'Some Hints on Furnishing our Australian Homes', which strongly advocated a swing to the new artistic style. The author 'Beryl' addresses herself chiefly to 'people who have not large amounts of money to spend, but who wish to have a pretty, tastefully arranged home, and to people

This Queensland interior contains many typical items: patterned linoleum and long-haired hearth-rug, and mantelpiece supporting a glass-domed clock and candelabra, behind which are spectacular fans.

who, living in the country, find a difficulty in knowing what are the newest and most appropriate materials that can be obtained in town'. Her recommendations are as fresh as they are clear. White (that is, cream) wood and cane make their entry while wallpaper makes its exit and much that was heavy and rich in atmosphere has been brushed aside. Surprisingly, the characteristic Victorian romantic notions of the drawing-room persist:

There are drawing-rooms that are idylls in luxurious comfort, poems in prettiness, from whence everything that savours too much of upholstery is banished, whilst all the surrounds and knick-knacks seem the result of natural growth; where one can see at once that some woman with loving hands has blended the grasses, leaves and flowers in the vases; where the latest magazine or newest book lies temptingly to one's hand on some small table; where all the chairs look inviting to sit or lounge in; where all the colours blend so harmoniously that it is difficult to tell how the effect is produced, only we feel that a subtle essence of everything that is pleasant in life of books, pictures, music, flowers and graceful women—is diffused through the room. This is the sort of drawing-room it should be our aim to have; this is the sort of room in which, on entering, we feel at once the truth of what Ruskin says, 'that art is an incarnation of fancy, and is a sort of petrified poetry, or concrete rhetoric'.[15]

'Beryl's' recipe for achieving a room of such charms was decidedly 'modern'. There is a retreat from the richer hues, to just pastels. Much that is superfluous in decoration is done away with and the painting of furniture is advocated enthusiastically. A strong note of practicality and economy is sounded for the first time. Furniture can be renovated, instead of being bought new. Lightness and prettiness are all important. Especially interesting is the entry of white (not a white as we know it but cream) as a colour for furniture, woodwork, mantelpiece and picture-frames. (Though the idea took a while to be accepted, by 1910 it was a regular style of decoration for drawing rooms.) A return to stiff-looking furniture emerges, countering the mid-Victorian voluptuous lines. The two sources of style embraced by 'Beryl' are the Adamesque and the French Empire, which seem to provide the perfect antidote to mid-Victorian 'excesses'. Both enjoyed a revival in popularity in the Edwardian period, especially the Adamesque in Australia.

In detail, 'Beryl's' recommendations are:

As regards the colours that should be used in a drawing-room, it is better to let one colour predominate, or rather be the key-note on which everything else is chosen. Blue, pale yellow, or terra-cotta are the most suitable colours. If blue or yellow are decided on, the furniture should

44

be in white wood, cane or satin wood; with a terra-cotta for the prevailing tone, Chippendale or Sheraton furniture, made in rosewood, looks extremely well. Wallpapers and cretonne, for hangings and curtains, can be obtained now in London in the same colouring and pattern, and the effect is very good, especially in a yellow and white drawing-room . . . There are many brocades and tapestries made nowadays, which are quite moderate in price and most useful in re-covering chairs and couches that are rather worn . . .

It is always best to have the boards of the drawing-room stained for about two or three feet all round; over the unstained part a fine matting or felt should be stretched and on this rugs may be laid, as in the hall. In former days curtains, with their heavy poles and valances, used to be a serious item in the furnishing of rooms; now the effect produced is far lighter and prettier, and the expense less than a quarter what it used to be. Nothing can be fresher looking or more suitable for a country house, in the climate, than curtains made of the art muslins, which are produced now in so many pretty patterns and shades; they should be made up with rings to run on a plain brass rod, and a straight valance of about eighteen inches deep, made of self-coloured muslin of the same shade as the curtains, and put on double, should hang from the top . . . If the walls are painted or distempered in a colour that corresponds with the tone of the curtains, and have a dado of Japanese paper lincrusta a shade darker, the foundation for a very pretty room will be laid; and even if new furniture cannot be indulged in, a good deal of the old can be renovated as I have suggested, with enamel paint and inexpensive Liberty silk or brocade . . .

FLOOR-
COVERINGS
CURTAINS

For a more ambitious sort of room — the illustration shows a new and very artistic style of panelling with an overmantel in the 'Empire' fashion. A piece of oval looking glass is let into the centre and the woodwork painted with white enamel paint. The 'cosy corners' here introduced near the fire-place can be made very useful, as well as comfortable, for the seats should be in the form of a lid like an ottoman, and inside can be put away newspapers, magazines, music books, etc., which it may be necessary to have at hand, but which do not look well in a drawing-room, when too much en evidence.

I am strongly opposed to having anything standing on the top of the piano, though there is a tendency to crowd it with photographs and ornaments. Nobody in these days need be without pictures on their walls, as beautiful engravings and mezzo-tints are produced at such a very moderate cost; these look very well on pale grey mounts, and framed in white frames. Suites of furniture are out of date in modern Drawing-rooms, but all the chairs and couches should be chosen with a view to their being first comfortable, and then artistic, and plenty of down cushions covered with Liberty silk and edged with frills, scattered about the couches.[16]

PIANO

PICTURES

FURNITURE

We leave Beryl here sounding the clarion in 1890 for all the changes that were implemented substantially a decade or so later in the wake of Victoria's reign.

CHAPTER TWO

The Dining-Room

Next to a well appointed drawing-room, the dining-room should be the best apartment in the house for social purposes. But its chief characteristics ought to be of a more sober and massive kind than becomes a chamber devoted to lighter and more feminine purposes.[1]

A VICTORIAN DINING-ROOM glowed with grandeur and dignity. The decoration of all its surfaces, the selection of furniture and all the trimmings were designed to create an effect of splendour and prosperity. In contrast to the brilliance of the drawing-room, massiveness, masculinity and magnificence dominated in the dining-room. A sense of purpose and confidence emanated from the powerful furniture, the calculated symmetry, the rich hangings and fulsome drapes. 'The sideboard cumbrous with plate'[2] and a battery of gilt-framed family portraits and landscapes in oils gave the room added lustre.

The dining-room expressed, in appropriately sombre tones, the more earnest and respectable values of the household. Being principally a man's domain, a place where he frequently entertained his friends, it was furnished with a full, rich and ostentatious hand. Its impact was calculated to be both warm and impressive, 'redolent of cheery comfort and prosperity'.[3]

How then was a dining-room decorated? What were its chief ingredients and how were they combined to achieve the desired effect? One author suggested that a dash of 'full-tones, rich, juicy colouring and decided treatment will give the necessary effect'.[4]

The key element in the decoration was the chimneypiece (that is, mantelpiece). It was usually dark in colour, either black, grey, brown or a combination of black with other colours. This was the cue for the colouring of the rest of the room, an element of red, green or brown tending to be continued in the wall colour. Marble was the favourite material for middle-class houses, lesser mortals contenting themselves generally with a 'marbled' chimneypiece or a simple varnished cedar one. Grander houses had a wider choice of materials and many house-owners opted for solid timber, carved into lofty overmantels. Mandeville Hall's dining-room is a typical example. Whatever the material though, the form and scale were impressive and the colour subdued.

The general colour of a dining-room tended towards one of two directions: either towards the warm shades of red, russet, ochre and sienna or towards green. Each was considered to be a good foil for furnishings and paintings and to be appropriately sombre and not a distraction. Splashes of gold, in the characteristically substantial cornice and ceiling decoration, as well as on the frames of the overmantel mirror and pictures, served to relieve the heaviness of the room.

A dado was considered highly desirable in the dining-room. As chairs were

Above: For sheer complexity, the ceiling in the dining-room of Ayers House, Adelaide, would have few rivals. The range of browns and soft greens, embellished with gold and stencilling, achieves subtlety and brilliance. The decoration was executed c. 1875.

Left: The dining-room at Mandeville Hall, Victoria, reflects much of Joseph Clarke's passion for England. The individually painted panels of hunting scenes create a frieze of great interest. A rich oak dado gives a solid foundation to the wall decoration.

At Rippon Lea, Victoria, the dining-room has a tantalizing combination of lavishly embossed wallpapers, velvet table cover, patterned carpet and curtains.

placed around the wall of the room, it was customary to have a dado treatment to the approximate height of the back of the chair and at that point to have a rail or border. It created a pleasing visual effect, giving a solid foundation to the wall above. The dado was painted or papered in relation to the walls above, but a good many shades darker.

the dark, dado takes from the bareness of a large room, and gives a coziness and furnished appearance which does not exist when you can see each piece of furniture clearly defined against the wall.[5]

Often the dado consisted of panelled design either in solid timber or in wallpaper or stencilled design. Sometimes a continuous heavily embossed paper was used. However, whatever the choice of materials, the effect of solidarity, subdivided by geometric lines, was sought. A geometric flavour often characterized the border above the dado—a motif of interlocking circles, or a continuous fret design were typical choices. The joinery would be painted in two shades of brown or perhaps black, rich red—brown or deep green. Alternatively, it may have been wood-grained.

Above the dado, the main wall surface stretched to the frieze. A likely choice for this section would have been a large damask pattern wallpaper or stencilled design or a similarly rich flowing design. Alternatively, it may have been simply painted a warm strong colour—an excellent foil for impressive paintings. The crowning glory of the walls was the frieze, which was often a softly flowing horizontal pattern with much embellishment. Sometimes the pattern took the form of a cresting, that is, a design with an upright aspect and 'crested' top.

The ceiling was generally painted a vellum or fawn colour in a depth to suit the walls. Corner designs of stencilling were used to relieve the plainness if complete decoration by stencilling was too costly. Alternatively, wallpapers were used, sometimes the Anaglypta type or one divided into geometric panels and painted and gilded.

An example of a wealthy man's dining-room decoration is provided by Wells:

The dado is covered with dark russet browns, and panelled with darker shades of the same. The wood-work is painted dark chestnut colour, the panels (i.e. in the doors) being decorated with a beautifully drawn Greek design in very thin lines of ivory colour, conveying the feeling of

inlaid work, and giving an effect of elegance and refinement. The walls are painted dark red, to form a good background for the splendid pictures which adorn this room. The frieze has a solid gold ground decorated with a conventionally treated floral design, the flowers being painted in shades of primrose-white, with hearts of citrine and delicate orange; the leaves are in shades of green, the whole being outlined in soft red.

The ground of the ceiling is a rich cream colour, all the decorations being hand-painted in soft harmonious tones of olive-green, primrose, orange and neutral tones of blue. The framework (i.e. the cornice) is mainly in lines of Persian red and gold. The general effect is warm and delicate.

The pillars at the end of the room are in dark chocolate and gold, the caps bronzed and lacquered, with the projections in gold; the whole being highly polished.[6]

An equally vivid account of the furnishings of a middle-class Australian dining-room in the 1870s is provided by the Melbourne furnisher and upholsterer, Rocke. His market lay chiefly with the average middle-class customer, whose taste for the conventional he encouraged, while offering a few alternatives in more exotic directions. The emphasis on 'fashions', especially 'Parisian fashions' is an obvious selling point.

A model dining-room would be about twenty feet by thirty feet long, and fifteen feet high, lighted by a triple window, curtained by silk rep, with Nottingham lace underneath. The cornice should be simply grand. The lace curtains should come from under a shaped fringe tipped with gold bullion. In summer time the curtains may be of cretonne and lace. The walls should be painted a neutral tint, in order to set off the pictures upon them, which are hung with flexible gold wire, fastened to gilt brass rods, terminating in rosettes, fixed close to the ceiling. If there are no pictures the dead space of the walls may be relieved by panels or medallions, in the centre of which are hand-painted heads or groups of flowers. A fashionable Parisian ornament consists of stuffed specimens of game, suspended by the feet, as though just shot. The carpet should be of a rather geometrical or close-figured [pattern] than of an open floriated pattern. At one end of the room is the fire-place, the mantel-piece of black marble, surmounted by a mirror seventy by fifty inches square, with a deep but not intricately moulded frame. On the mantel-piece should stand a massive pendule of porphyry, candelabra of green bronze, and vases, and statuettes. On each side of the fire-place should be bell-pulls (bell-handles are unfashionable), terminating in a heavy rosette or tassel. At the opposite end of the

Beautifully suggestive of the pleasure of fine food is this stencilled ceiling at Glenleigh near Sydney. Fish, fowl, game and deer are painted in panels in each corner.

Overleaf: A profusion of wallpapers in the dining-room of Yallum Park in South Australia, with the boldest of colours, including mauve, green and pink, converging on the cornice. The sheer extravagance of papers, dados, borders and friezes achieves a cohesive and powerful effect. The chairs, table and leather-covered sofa are the original furnishings. The venetian blinds are of wood and the pelmet is of pressed brass.

49

Symmetry and masculinity predominate in the dining-room of Ranfurlie, Victoria. The heavily carved furniture is well-matched by the bold flowing frieze above plain walls and an embossed dado.

The dining-room at Tudor Lodge, Hawthorn, Melbourne, in 1891, has moved far from middle-class decoration to a highly personalized, artistic and eclectic style.

Simple bentwood chairs around a modest-sized table form the hub of this homely Queensland dining-room. Note the painted timber walls, simple drapes and typical light-fittings.

chamber should be placed a massive side-board or buffet of mahogany (if the rest of the suite be of that wood), not too elaborately carved, but polished so as to bring out the rich grain in full lustre, and with a mirror back. On this buffet (Note a) may be displayed testimonial plates, race or regatta cups, silver services, and the like. The dining-table (Note b), supported on massive fluted legs, terminating in carved claws, should be fitted at each end with patent screws, for the purpose of its elongation or abbreviation at pleasure. An open dinner-waggon on castors should be near the door. If a side table is used, it should be very richly carved. A three-winged book-case, sufficiently ornamented to avoid the imputation of plainness, would complete an ordinary list of dining-room appurtenances. If the wall space is not wanted for pictures, one sofa or two couches may be introduced. These must correspond with the chairs — eight ordinary dining-room chairs, two easy chairs, and a lounge chair — all of which must be covered with dull grained or smooth polished morocco. Their pattern can be chosen from a vast variety of designs, some antique, some mediaeval, some intensely modern, but all substantial. It is not a bad plan to have the leather stretched smooth, without tufts or buttons, in which case the backs can be imprinted with a monogram or coat of arms in gold. Large brass bosses or studs should mark the line where the stuffing joins the body of the chair. The table-cloth should be of the superfine material known as billiard cloth (not necessarily green), matching the furniture covering, and edged with gold-covered braiding.

We also supply several striking varieties of patterns in oak suites, which, when moulded upon a Gothic design, give to an apartment an antique air, which, when combined with the presence of every modern appurtenance of comfort, is very impressive. Green, or blue, or pink trimmings match best with oak, and when an extreme air of lightness and richness is required, pink trimmed with blue will be found to produce it. Most of our oak furniture is deprived of an objectionable air of prevalent yellowness by the introduction, for shading purposes, of panels and inlaid ornaments of dark brown bog oak.

We commence a new paragraph in order to call attention to our very latest novelty in oaken furniture, and it is something very superb. The light colour of the wood is made to serve as the background of ebony and different coloured inlayings, mostly of a very choice Pompeiian character. Some Gothic book-cases lately arrived present a new form of decoration, in the shape of diamond panels, with bosses in the centres.

Post scriptum — Should it be arranged that there may be smoking in the dining-room, it would be advisable to furnish it with a series of circular footstools, in oak or mahogany, with highly ornamental tops, which, when taken off, discover disguised spittoons.

(a) *Dining-room sideboards are usually designed to be imposing and grand, rather than gay and ornamental. In some, however, there is a luxurious display of fine carving and a frequency of ornaments that accord with a very rich general effect. In the Gothic oak style the latter is a frequent case. We have them as plain or as elaborate as you choose.*

(b) *Dining-tables may be oval or square, to suit the room or rest of the furniture. We have hall-tables expressly designed to contain in their backs the spare leaves of the dining-table.*[7]

The same style of decoration and furnishing of a dining-room is described, though somewhat contemptuously, by Twopeny, in his account of Australian houses. He first looks at Muttonwool's dining-room, a representative specimen of the upper middle class:

We will now go into the dining-room, which is probably the best furnished room in the house. It is not easy to make a dining-room look out of joint provided you are not particular about the cost, though there is a very wide margin between the decent and the handsome. The upholstery is much the same as in an ordinary upper middle-class house in England — sofa, sideboard, chiffonier, two easy and eight or ten upright chairs in cedar frames and covered with leather, marble mantelpiece and clock, Louis XVI glass, and a carpet which is at any rate better than the drawing-room one.[8]

Conformity to a furnishing formula was apparently universal. The furnishing of a more modest house, still middle class but not affluent, revealed the same pieces of furniture though the quality was reduced. Cedar is the predominent wood for the house, which is a 'typical eight-roomed cottage':

The real living-room of the house is the dining-room, which is therefore the best furnished, and on a tapestry carpet are a leather couch, six balloon-back carved chairs, two easy-chairs, a chiffonier, a side-table, and a cheap chimney-glass.[9]

One rung below this home-owner were the cottages of clerks, shop-keepers and the like, whose income would have been approximately £300 to £400 a year. Where means were reduced the 'style is the same, but the quantity and quality inferior'; 'the dining-room furniture is covered with horse-hair instead of leather, and so on'.[10]

Further down the line, in a simple rented cottage the drawing-room and dining-room merge into one more-modest unit, the parlour. In a cosy compacted fashion, the same furnishing formula survives: the horsehair cedar couch, the lady's and gentleman's chairs, four balloon chairs, a chiffonier, and a round table, with central pillar and carved claws, from which family dinners would be taken. The parlour of a humble labourer is frugal. Cane-seated chairs are used instead of the upholstered cedar ones. Another economy is in the rocking chair, made of maple, which supplants the lady's and gentleman's chairs. Cedar couch and central table remain and perhaps a built-in cedar cupboard beside the fireplace replaces the chiffonier.

Just as the scale of furnishing reflected the means of the owner or occupier of the house, so too did it govern the mode of surface decoration in the various levels of society. The notions of dining-room grandeur were adhered to throughout the layers of fashion-conscious Victorians. For all but the most affluent levels of the middle class, a great dependence on wallpaper appears, with abundant designs for all parts of walls and ceilings in the dining-room. Showy floral, elaborate papers offered the perfect solution of impressive decoration at a reasonable price. Wardlow is a splendid example of this style of decoration. The more simple stencilled designs were also in demand, especially for ceilings. Instead of having the elaborate panoramic ceilings that the wealthy could afford, the pragmatic middle-class home-owner contented himself with the next best thing—one- or two-colour stencilled designs judiciously placed on the ceiling, as at Rouse Hill House or Westella.

Below this level in society, where the means to decorate were further diminished, the one vestige of dining-room status was the dado. The presence of a wallpaper dado, or soft-wood panelling constituting a dado, gave some particular dignity to a room. Above it could be a plain painted wall, the mere use of a dado being suggestive of the appropriate formality.

By 1890 much of the conformity of dining-rooms was swept away. The extreme sombreness of the dining-room had become objectionable. According to 'Beryl', writing for housewives in her 'Art in the Home' column:

It is an accepted canon of good taste that the general tone and colouring of the dining-room should be darker than that of the drawing-room. In the last generation this was carried to an extreme, and the dining-room, under what Miss Thackeray calls 'the reign of terror of mahogany' must have been anything but a cheerful looking apartment. Fortunately for us, much better taste prevails nowadays; light oak and walnut have driven out mahogany in all its massiveness; and though there is a great taste now for old dark oak for dining-room furniture, yet it becomes only a pleasant contrast to the cheerful coloured walls, curtains and carpets.[11]

After such a statement it comes as somewhat of a surprise that she recommends:

Olive greens, golden browns, dark terra-cottas, or Indian red are the colours most suitable for the walls and curtains. In the way of wall decoration there is nothing better than wood-panelling.[12]

Her chief recommendations are that the general clutter of the room, especially of the sideboard, be reduced and that a degree of lightness in the timbers be introduced. The shape of things to come in the post-Victorian era.

A dining-room corner from Terry and Oakden's book, What to Build and How to Build it, *published in 1886.*

A dining-room corner from Terry and Oakden's book, What to Build and How to Build it, *published in 1886.*

The Honourable S. Winter Cooke of Murndal, near Hamilton, Victoria, dining with his family in 1901. The table is lit by candles in an elaborate fitting, through which flowers and branches are entwined, cascading to the table arrangement. Kerosene lamps are also on the table and sideboard.

Above: The magnificent room at Woolmers, Tasmania, derives much of its atmosphere from the rich red flock wallpaper used without either dado or frieze. Lustrous mahogany, gleaming silver and sumptuous paintings complete the effect of warmth and opulence. Particularly rare is the central light-fitting—a counterbalanced, five-branched fusion of kerosene lamps. The room was decorated in 1859.

Right: Using a theme of greens and blues, this typical middle-class dining-room at Westella in Hawthorn, Victoria, was built in 1888. Stencilwork embellishes the ceiling and accents the lines of the cornice.

Above: The recreated dining-room at Oxford (formerly Friesia), Hawthorn, Victoria, in which imitation leather wallpaper was used for the dado, a timber rail placed above it and the walls painted a Pompeiian red.

Left: Both for its decorative value and as a portent of plenty, the pomegranate was chosen for the chief motif in the decoration of the dining-room at Glenleigh, near Penrith in New South Wales. A stylized arrangement of the plant has been formed into a full stencilled wall design. A deep pink dado provides a base for the decoration and carries an extra border at mid-point. Until recently, this wall decoration was covered with paint, which had to be carefully sanded and scraped off.

CHAPTER THREE

The Entrance Hall

In a picture filled with decorative interest, we see an eminent Victorian businessman, Mr Septimus Miller, and his family in their mansion, Cantala, which still stands in Caulfield, Victoria.

With a rather extraordinary use of potted ferns, this entrance has an almost glade-like feeling. The walls are hung with an imitation timber panelled wallpaper, while the floor and stairs are covered with bordered linoleum runners.

Directly you set foot inside the front door you begin to judge the character of the inmates.[1]

THE ENTRANCE HALL, far from being a mere passage from the front door to the various rooms, was considered to be a most significant area, worthy of careful attention and the best available materials and techniques. 'Effort should be made here to convey an impression of comfort, warmth and homeliness.'[2] It was felt that the much valued qualities of 'harmony and repose' should here first impress themselves upon the visitor. The general tone should be one of tranquillity and warmth. 'The colouring of the hall should be low in tone and richly quiet in effect, suggesting comfort and even opulence, but forming a simple contrast to the entertaining, and other rooms opening out of it.'[3]

A typically decorated middle-class entrance hall was either pleasantly warm in colour, using a terracotta or even a Pompeiian red, or softly cool, using shades of green. 'Halls and stair-cases should be of some warm quiet tones of colouring such as reds or greens which are not positive colours. They provide a relief to the eyes after the glare of daylight.'[4]

The dado was always coloured in deeper shades of the wall colour. Wallpapers in matching combinations for dado, wall space and frieze were often used. The dado, if not the entire wall, was often varnished to allow regular cleaning. A very popular treatment can be seen in the photograph of Wardlow. A combination of papers has been used, based on a stylized flower motif, which is open and trailing above the dado. Varnishing gives it a rich, glossy look. Alternatively, walls could be marbled or made to look like granite either in paint or wallpaper. Yallum Park is a fine example of the latter.

The walls generally had a frieze beneath the cornice and a dado beneath the middle wall space. The dado followed the rake of the hand-rail in the staircase. A wooden mounted rail or special band separated the dado from the wall space. The cornice was coloured to connect the ceiling and walls. In its entirety, it framed the ceiling. The darkest colour was at the base, with shades becoming lighter towards the ceiling: always with the deepest ones darker than the general wall colour.

The ceiling was usually painted a neutral shade of light vellum (beige), light blue, or buff, related to the colouring of the walls. It was often decorated with a stencilled ornament that was not necessarily expensive. Alternatively, the ceiling may have been papered, keeping the shade neutral in tone, with one of the many papers used for ceilings. A lattice type of pattern using simple geometric designs in very subdued harmonizing colours would have been a likely choice. A little gilding introduced in small spots and thin lines gave definition to the leading forms of the design and had a generally enriching effect.

Etchings, autotypes and engravings were hung on the walls. The hallway was also an appropriate place to display trophies of the hunt—foxes' heads, stags' heads and the like. Rouse Hill House displays a splendid trio of mounted stag heads. Stuffed birds in a case may also have found a place. Statuary of all kinds enjoyed commanding positions along the walls, especially on either side of an archway. Palms with gracefully sweeping fronds draped the thoroughfare.

The woodwork was painted in one or more shades of maroon or other rich brown colours, or alternatively wood-grained. Marbling over plaster was another possibility in grand houses. Steps of the staircase were stained a deep brown colour and varnished.

The carpets, known as runners, were of a Turkish or similar design, with a central pattern and border along each side in strong colours. Encaustic tiles would be a likely alternative treatment for floors, being both practical and decorative. Essential furnishing was a hallstand, either timber or cast-iron bronzed, and two or more matching non-upholstered chairs. A small hall table with a drawer and perhaps a shield on the back panel was often included in the entrance-hall furnishing.

An excellent example of an elaborate entrance hall decorated by stencilling survives at Mintaro. It is a rare example of such completeness. From the floor to the ceiling the surfaces are decorated by coordinated stencil designs. In colouring, it is a combination of soft greens on the walls, with rich yellows and browns on a cream background on the ceiling. Clusters of fluted yellow scagliola columns create a gentle contrast with the predominant green of the walls.

The dado of Mintaro's hall carries a powdering, that is, a pattern of isolated motifs without a continuous line of connection, based on the fleur de lis. A remarkable border is applied above the dado. It consists of bands, painted and shaded in various tones of brown and yellow to suggest a moulded piece of timber. The illusion of polished timber is only shattered by running one's hand down the wall. Above the border a beautiful Renaissance-style diaper pattern has been applied, also by stencilling. A shallow frieze completes the wall treatment. Lines of richly embellished cornice frame the ceiling. The hall in its entirety is an fine example of typical mid-Victorian Renaissance-inspired decoration.

The hallway in a simple cottage would aspire to the same atmosphere of restfulness and softness as its middle- and upper-class counterparts. The scale and architectural pretensions may be minimal but the same colours and decorative approach would prevail. Stencilling of a simple kind would be a likely choice. Perhaps a plain band of deep colour, rich red or green, would suffice for the dado, with a modest painted line of demarcation above it. Above this may be a plain wall, topped by a frieze, the most elaborate element to be found. A classical design of stylized flowers, perhaps in two or three colours, might be chosen, in all about 350 millimetres deep. With little or no cornice above the frieze, the ceiling would be framed in two or three painted bands echoing the predominant tones of the walls. Modest corner ornaments would complete the ceiling decoration. A small lantern with coloured glass panels was popular for hallways.

If a combination of wallpaper and painted techniques were selected, a likely choice would be one of the imitation papers. Made to convey the impression of coursed stone, or panelled timber or speckled granite, they added a fantastic dimension to wall decoration. Working men's diminutive entrance halls were transformed into miniature replicas of their grander models. Even the rough boards of the early Captain John Mills Cottage at Port Fairy, Victoria, carried a granite paper, complete with coursing, in its entrance hallway after 1854. The incongruity of such a choice apparently had no bearing on the matter, so great was the pleasure in the effect. On a grander scale, the entrance hall of Rouse Hill House has marbling. In this case the treatment is painted on, also with coursing to give the proper effect, and the result is visually impressive. An English country squire's residence is discernible in the style of decoration and furnishing.

A rich woody magnificence characterizes the vestibule of Goathland, the late Victorian mansion of Sir Malcolm and Lady McEachern, photographed in 1901.

A real mixture of greenery, drapery, statuary and horn(ery) make the entrance hall at Blair Athole, at Brighton, Victoria, a splendid specimen of its kind!

Right: The entrance hall or vestibule at Mintaro, near Romsey, Victoria, bears testimony to the skill of Victorian decorators, such as C. Brettschneider, who carried out the work. It shows excellence in the arts of stencilling and marbling, as well as talent for blending colour and architectural arrangement. Panels of Minton tiles divide the floor area into panels. The stencilled lines and shading above the dado cleverly suggest a timber rail. Doors to the drawing-room and dining-room are wood-grained to imitate oak.

Above: The stairway of Glenhope, near Sydney, emphasizes the richly carved timberwork of the late Victorian period. It carries the original decoration, including a stencilled frieze. The wall below the rail was originally a deep blue–green.

Right: The entrance hall at Woolmers, Tasmania, bears all the hallmarks of early Victorian decoration. The scale is squat but spacious, the architectural embellishments such as the brown-coloured Greek revival cornice are minimal.

Far right: The untouched entrance hall at Yallum Park, South Australia, has a wealth of decoration: rich oak wood-graining, etched glass, imitation-marble papered walls and ceiling wallpapers.

CHAPTER FOUR

The Library

Captain J. P. Chirnside standing before his collection of native weapons decorating the chimneybreast of his smoking-room at The Manor, Werribee, Victoria.

Note the draped chimneypiece in this 1901 picture of Sir Simon Fraser in his library at Norla, Toorak, Victoria.

Libraries are the wardrobes of literature, where men, properly informed, might bring forth something for ornament, much for curiosity, and more for use.[1]

THE VICTORIANS, EVEN THE MOST HUMBLE, took great pride in the development of their era. The success of Queen Victoria as a leader of one of the greatest empires in history, gave the Victorians a powerful sense of purpose and importance, reflected in their architecture and decoration. Many were fascinated by the scientific, archaeological, engineering and other discoveries that took place during Queen Victoria's reign. A pleasure in knowledge of such spheres of advancement were to be shared with and demonstrated to a gentleman's friends and colleagues. The appropriate room to display such collections and items of interest was the library. Hobbyists, collectors, diarists, and men of letters were very active in a time when the pursuit of knowledge was so keenly followed. The decorative treatment of the typical library was 'sober and thoughtful' and tertiary colouring could be used to good effect.

The decoration should not court attention, but it should be so studied in form and meaning as to lead the mind back by suggestion to books. Quotations and mottoes will not be out of place specially if they embody the ideas and principles of the master of the house.[2]

Here was the ideal room for a man to demonstrate his love of historicity and erudition. The architectural forms of the room as well as the decoration should indicate a knowledge of the classical world as well as contemporary developments.

Not all Victorian gentlemen had a house large enough to include a library, so it was a decided feather in the cap of a gentleman if he could attain this achievement and refinement.

To assert that no house is complete without a room set apart for a library, would be an impertinence. Not every man of wealth has had opportunities of cultivating literary tastes; and a library for mere show is a piece of presumptuous hypocrisy. Moreover, in the case of a professional man, his library is not necessarily kept in his house, and the dining-room book-case may answer all the purposes of himself and family. Should you, however, set apart a room for studious and bookish purposes, there is not one in which your higher characteristics can be better displayed.[3]

The library in a gentleman's residence was frequently located off the hallway, to the left as one entered the house. It was a room of generally subdued tones, in marked contrast to the drawing-room, which was usually opposite. The walls were the background for rare prints and etchings, so it was often painted, or if papered, it was given some old rich leather effect. Predominant colours were browns and ochres, with some gold. The ceiling and cornice would be coloured to match the wall colours. The woodwork, as in the dining-room, was usually dark in tone and embellished with stencilling. A brown, black or otherwise dark-coloured fireplace was standard for the library.

Books and their large, handsome cases were an essential part of this room, echoing the mellow browns and soft textures of the other decorative elements. The whole room was arranged to convey an impression of warmth and richness, with at least a hint of seriousness and intellectual substance.

An ideal library is described by Rocke in 1874:

It is a tall, spacious room, with an astral lamp dependent from the central ceiling ornament; the ceiling cornice of a richly ornate scroll pattern; the walls stained of a warmish brown, relieved by extremely narrow vertical stripes, save where the wall space is occupied by gorgeously carved Gothic bookcases of oak (Note a) or choice pictures; and a carpet (Note b) of comparatively minute-figured pattern to match. Over the antique marble piece (the mantel chimney-piece covered with velvet edged with a deep hanging fringe) is a group of statuary in miniature, flanked by vases of Etruscan mould. Busts of the great dead have their stands on brackets variously situated, and care is taken that the fitting minor conveniences of life are at hand. Two tables, containing nests of small drawers, and carved to correspond with the bookcases, have places at opposite ends of the room; they are covered with smooth morocco, of a cobalt hue, as also are the chairs, some of which are fauteuils *and others ordinary dining-room chairs. In every case the morocco is edged with bands of gold. Silken curtains, falling from behind a deeply-fringed cornice, veil the windows; and the apartment, if it could speak, would murmur the lines of Wordsworth:*
'Books we know
Are a substantial world, both pure and good:
Round these, with tendrils strong as flesh and blood,
Our pastime and our happiness will grow'.

(a) Whether the fittings of the room should be of oak or mahogany depends much upon the prevailing colour of the bindings of the books on the shelves.

(b) A library carpet should always be of an unobstrusive pattern and subdued tint. Carpets of that description are frequently required for Government and other offices, and we have made ample provision for giving purchasers every variety of choice.[4]

Any attempt at restoration or redecoration of a library should endeavour to capture the essential atmosphere of this room. The leathery charm of books should pervade it, against a background of rich colours and lustrous timbers. An air of easy comfort, warmth and intellectual adventure should emanate from the room.

A restful room, thought to be a smoking-room at Mt Sturgeon, an Armytage family property in Victoria.

Above: It would be hard to imagine a more sporty, colourful or original room than this library, formerly the school-room at Eeyeuk, a homestead built in 1875 near Terang, Victoria. The walls are decorated with varnished newspaper and magazine cuttings. Alexander Dennis mounted the collection of birds.

Left: The predominant green–browns of the wallpaper and frieze in the library at Meningoort, Victoria, are picked up in the stencilled corner ornament of the ceiling and contrasted with bands of a warm pinkish brown in the cornice.

Far left: The impressive qualities of the Victorian library are well shown in this example at Meningoort, the McArthur property at Camperdown, Victoria. The decoration, which was carried out in the 1870s for John McArthur.

CHAPTER FIVE

The Billiard-Room

One curious feature of Victorian houses is the increasingly large and sacrosanct male domain, an expansion in size and time of the after-dinner aspect of the Georgian dining room. The nucleus of the male preserve was the billiard room.[1]

Captioned My Favourite Shot, *this picture shows Sir Samuel Gillott at Edensor, Fitzroy, Victoria, having a game of billiards with* Melbourne Punch *writer 'Lauderdale'.*

A typical wallpaper treatment is used in the billiard-room of Bronte at Brighton, Victoria, the home of lawyer Thomas Prout Webb.

ABOVE THE DOORWAY TO EVERY ROOM at Osborne House, Queen Victoria's residence, were the letters V and A entwined. The one exception was the doorway to the smoking-room, over which there loomed a solitary A—proof, if ever it were required, that females were excluded from such rooms.

The male domain was a favourite part of the Victorian gentleman's residence. For some fortunate fellows on country estates, it consisted of a generous suite of rooms to relax in with their friends. The billiard-room was its hub. In simpler houses, a gentleman contented himself with the essential billiard-room.

From the Georgian practice of excluding females from the after-dinner conversation, the notion of a territory for gentlemen evolved naturally. In the highly conventionalized existence of the Victorians, so much was considered unsuitable for a nicely-brought-up lady to see, to hear, to read or to talk about, that there remained little alternative but for the gentlemen to take sanctuary in their own precinct in order to enjoy a free and easy time.

Although the game of billiards had been known for centuries, it took the particular impetus of the Victorian era to raise it to the level of a national pastime. Moreover, it became a pastime worthy of a distinctive room, generating its own special ethos. The billiard-room filled a gaping hole in the complex fabric of Victorian life. Its attraction lay not so much in the game of billiards as in the pleasure of casting off the shackles imposed by mixed company. It provided a sanctum to which gentlemen could retire and indulge in some of their favourite activities of which, one suspects, playing billiards was a minor one. More significant perhaps was the opportunity it afforded them to enjoy 'the fragrant weed'. Smoking, though made fashionable by Prince Albert and later by the Prince of Wales, was not accepted socially and therefore remained shrouded in some kind of fascinating masculine mystique.

Although the billiard-room offered the ideal solution to the Victorian gentleman's need for privacy with his smoking, joking, gregarious companions. It provided the perfect escape-valve for the restrictive conditions of large households that were often crowded with females of all kinds, including spinster sisters and their like, as well as offspring. Some houses had separate smoking-rooms or small tower-rooms reserved for such purposes. St Agnes at Kyneton in Victoria, Labassa and Woolmers have their own smoking-rooms.

As the enthusiasm for segregated quarters gained momentum, billiard-rooms emerged in new houses. Many of the simpler early Victorian houses were extended to include a recreational wing or at least a billiard-room, as a male enclave. The decoration of these rooms reflected a zealous bias towards male assertiveness.

Rocke's advice on smoking-rooms, which might well have applied to billiard-rooms, decreed that 'the point is to give the chamber an easy and somewhat luxurious air, coupled with a tone denoting that it is not devoted to the purposes of the softer sex.'

Of particular importance was the masculine decor of the room. All that upheld the image of masculine supremacy was displayed. Scenes from the rural sports, portraits of horses and trophies of the hunt adorned the walls. Deer heads were favourites. Almost as popular were large fan-shaped arrangements of guns, swords and spears. Paintings of all kinds, sometimes in great abundance, completed the wall decoration.

A long, buttoned leather couch usually stretched along one wall on a raised platform, offering the spectators a commanding and comfortable view of the game. In the centre, handsome and massive on its mighty mahogany or oak legs, stood the billiard-table. Suspended on angular brass rods, a flotilla of shaded lights focused on the verdant brilliance of the felt. In contrast, the rest of the room was subdued and softly hazy. Around the table it was customary for the floor to be covered with a patterned runner, often of linoleum, which, apart from its practical purpose, visually served to reinforce the typical rectangularity of the billiard-room. The combination of lustrous timbers, soft leather, smooth felt and gleaming billiard balls formed the room's distinctive textural flavour. By comparison the treatment of wall and ceiling surfaces was generally simple. Painted surfaces predominated, usually in soft greens, brown and ochres. Wallpaper was used rather sparingly but was by no means out of place.

In Australia, there are few survivors of the Victorian billiard-room. Most are unrecognizable as the impressive rooms they once were and many have undergone painful conversions to rooms of a more utilitarian value. One which has fortunately been preserved substantially is at Boree Cabonne at Cudal, near Orange in New South Wales. It was built in 1897 for Lancelot Noel Smith and has undergone only a minor alteration in the treatment of the wall surface since that time. The present deep red wallpaper is thoroughly compatible with the character of the room and differs only slightly from the original. In its furnishing, the room is original even to the neat little corner wash-basin, in which the players washed their hands before the game. As a billiard-room it is not among the most fanciful or exotic but it has a straightforward quality of pleasing proportions and handsome decor. Especially enjoyable is the collection of engravings it houses, hung at a comfortably low level. With its attractive woody warmth, it is richly evocative of a favourite Victorian pastime.

Another fine billiard-room that has survived the rigours of the twentieth century is at Eynesbury near Melton, Victoria. It was built in 1888 as an addition

The typical masculine decorations are displayed in the billiard-room of Everard Brown's Coroorooke House at Colac, Victoria.

The billiard-room at Blair Athole, Brighton, Victoria, the home of Mr and Mrs W. H. Felstead, photographed for Melbourne Punch *in 1901.*

Mars Buckley's billiard-room at Beaulieu, Toorak, Victoria, is resplendent with stags' heads. The walls have a magnificent frieze, a plain painted filling section and a heavily embossed dado.

Above: The late Victorian billiard-room at Boree Cabonne, near Orange in New South Wales, has a traditional character, with a modern frieze. Built in 1895 for Noel Lancelot Smith, the room has a warm atmosphere enhanced by the engravings on the walls.

Opposite page: The billiard-room at Yallum Park, South Australia. A bevy of striking papers, zany cornice lines, vibrant colours and a dazzling array of patterns on walls, floor and ceiling set it among the most spectacular of rooms.

to a good-looking bluestone house belonging to the Staughton family. Apart from its generally pleasing proportions, the room's most dazzling feature is the swirling soft-hued paper covering the walls. It is a bold and gorgeous aesthetic-style design based on the peony rose in shades of brown on a shimmering blue ground. The ceiling is tinted pale blue and a pair of ceiling roses are painted in blue and off-white to harmonize. In each corner of the ceiling a simple stencilled design has been executed in a deeper blue. Above the deep wallpaper frieze, the cornice is painted in shades of blue, beige and off-white to link wall with ceiling. Apart from the billiard-table, only the buttoned leather spectators' couch remains of the original furnishing of the room.

In the restoration of billiard-rooms, one must look at Werribee Park where particular effort has been expended on authentic redecoration. It captures the warmth and leatheriness of the typical Victorian examples, as well as much of the sporty embellishments and distinctive symmetry.

66

CHAPTER SIX

The Bedroom

Two panels of original decoration are revealed in the bedroom at The Abbey, Sydney. True to the Gothic theme of the house, the wardrobe and hand-basin are designed in the same style, as well as the window and archway.

Custom, a love of reasonable luxury, and a thousand and one individual ideas and associations lead people generally to make their chief bedroom—an apartment most pleasing to the eye and every sense that has aught to do with it.[1]

ALTHOUGH THE PRINCIPAL BEDROOM was not a prestigious public room, it was considered highly significant as a sanctum for the lady of the house, especially if she did not have an adjoining boudoir in which to recline and relax. As it was customary for a Victorian lady to spend a good deal of time in the bedroom, it was decorated and furnished very much according to her needs. An atmosphere somewhat akin to the drawing-room prevailed, with an emphasis on femininity and delicacy. Colours usually favoured were pastels, the warmer hues being used to cheer up a room of chilly aspect; conversely the greens and blues were used to cool a room with too warm an aspect.

Much attention was paid, in theory at least, to hygienic decorative treatments in bedrooms. Some writers went so far as to discourage the use of wallpapers on the basis that they harboured harmful insects as well as dust. Many ladies, however, must have remained unconvinced or unconcerned, as many bedrooms were wallpapered and the samples of this type of paper remained abundant. A typical recommendation was:

[The bedroom] treatment must be clearly, airy and cheerful, not too insistent, and forming a good contrast to the staircase and landings. Purity of tint and freshness of colour will attain this end . . . The painted work must be made easily washable, and all crevices likely to hold dust or to encourage moth or insect life should be scrupulously filled up.[2]

In keeping with its peaceful purposes, the decorative patterns of the bedroom were chosen to be unobtrusive and pleasant: 'Patterns of disturbing element and pronounced line, or of an angular tendency, should be discarded.'[3] Soft floral designs, not too sharply defined, would have been very likely choices. Some lovely examples remain at Mintaro.

The range of wallpapers varied considerably from the early part of the Victorian era to the years of greatest expansion in the 1880s. Modest floral bouquets arranged against a muted striped background were popular from the beginning. An especially splendid and bold example survived from 1859 under many layers of paper in a bedroom at Clarendon Terrace, East Melbourne. Again the broad vertical stripe is alternated with the beautiful, almost fragrant flowers that appear fresh-picked. As the period advanced, the more entwined floral designs asserted their popularity for bedrooms as much as they did for drawing-rooms. Along with the extra fullness of wall decoration came the rich swathing of the bed-head and windows in sumptuous soft fabrics and equally luxurious upholstered furniture. A predilection for comfort and prettiness became apparent. A matching suite of furniture consisting of wardrobe, dressing-table, chest of drawers and washstand formed the basis of the bedroom furniture. Lighter coloured woods such as pine or oak were favoured though cedar and mahogany were also used. Several easy chairs and a couch were essentials.

Rocke's remarks on decorating the bedroom outline the general trends:

This Queensland bedroom reinforces the notion of the room as a place of quiet pastimes, such as reading and writing. The blinds are highly decorative.

Having coloured your walls with a design that is not obtrusive, but nevertheless has a dash of chastened richness about it, you next choose your carpet . . . We will indicate a few bed-room carpet patterns, all of the requisite subdued type. Here are oaken scrolls picked out with white, and delicately shaded, that would accord well with mahogany or cedar furniture; or light green patterns alternated by white, cerise, and crimson, relieved with delicate sprays of oak, admirably adapted to oak or pine furniture; or, at your pleasure, you can choose a deep claret scroll on a broad white background; or the styles known as mottled green, granite green, moss green, drab moss, &c. Kamptulicon mats should lie before the washstands.

You decide upon your bedstead, and at this point the fact that you live in a warm climate cuts you off from the many luxuries attachable to the gorgeously carved and decorated four-poster. Primarily, considerations of health, and, secondarily, the fear of encouraging insect life, cause it to be laid down as a rule that your bedstead must be of iron, or brass, or both; and experience points to the half-tester as probably possessing more advantages to Australians than any other form . . . The bedstead in this instance is made of painted iron — that being the best and most durable material — except at the foot, where the rail consists of fine scroll-work, reaching about twenty inches above the bed, and extending below to within a few inches from the ground . . . Many bedsteads have the testers and bed-heads also of brass moulded in arabesque, Gothic, or other designs. In our opinion, however, the whole of the bed-head and bed-top should be hid in drapery, leaving exposed only the brass foot-rail, which we would have lined of the DRAPERY OVER BEDSTEAD *same material as the other trimmings. These may be of pure white dimity, ribbed, figured, or plain, or of choice cretonne or of plain silk . . . If silk is used it may be fluted both at the lining of the gilt foot-rail and at the bed-head, and the curtains may be simply divided across from the top to hang down on each side, or you may have a separate canopy lightly trimmed with coloured fringe. The valances must match, of course . . . The window curtains must correspond with* WINDOW CURTAINS *those of the bed, and hang from a pole, over which there may be a cornice . . . But of all these materials for bed-hangings silk is the most fashionable and luxurious. You may have it of blushing cerise, of a light shade of green, of French grey (we have this colour in exquisite tints), of pink, of azuline blue, or of sky blue. As a rule, white silk is somewhat too delicate for the purpose. At the foot-rail the silk should be fluted or plaited, and so also at the bed-head, unless you prefer that that should be tufted or buttoned, and resemble padding. The drapery overhead should be small, and trimmed with Paris fringe. The corresponding silken window curtains may have white lace ones underneath. Another description of bed furniture is purely French. It consists wholly of Swiss or Nottingham lace, with even the counterpane (lined, however) of the same material. Whether your mattress shall have springs, or whether you will lie on hair or feathers, are matters of taste . . . Except in the case of lace hangings, you may have your counterpane of eider-down, quilted with silk or other material, or of white marcella; or, it may be, you will prefer a white 'royal' quilt, with knitted fringed borders.*

Will you have your bedroom furniture of mahogany, of cedar, of oak, or of pine? Our FURNITURE *colonial Huon pine is an unsurpassable material, but colonial cabinet-makers, as a rule, though they can carve, can rarely inlay, and in some of the most perfect designs for light-coloured bedroom suites the art of inlaying is plentifully availed of. For instance, we refer to one which is wonderfully handsome and effective. Its material is simple pitch pine, but the various articles are modelled in a mediaeval fashion, with trefoils, quatre-foils, cinque-foils, bevelling, and bronze 'fixings', and every detail of the pattern is followed by inlaid and stained lines of ebony and silver. It is a triumph of workmanship and taste. When oak is used, it is frequently inlaid with bog oak of a dark brown shade, in order to give variety to the design. Mahogany and cedar are sometimes thought too dark for a bed-chamber. The slab of the washstand ought to be of pure white marble, or tesselated with encaustic tiles.*

. . . The dressing-table may be constructed in different ways. Two wings, each with a DRESSING TABLE *marble top and full of drawers, may have between them a full-length chevel-glass; or you may content yourself with a swing-glass on a level with the table, in order that the space underneath*

Right: Bands of stencilling and painted work take the place of the usual plasterwork and wallpaper decoration in this bedroom at Glenleigh, New South Wales. The original decoration, was until recently covered by many layers of paint. Careful scraping back revealed the designs and subtle colours of the work. Fresh stencils were then cut and the original work re-executed.

Far right: A Victorian bedroom recreated at Oxford in Hawthorn, Victoria, showing some of the usual pieces of furniture and the mode of painting joinery to blend with wallpaper.

Below right: Modest houses, such as Rosemount at Castlemaine, Victoria, had simple decoration. A neat frieze has been used, but a timber beading supplants the usual cornice and the dado is dispensed with. The pine ceiling, painted to complement the wallpaper, creates a good effect. The decoration was carried out in 1888.

Far right: A bedroom filled with the personality of a fine Victorian lady, Mrs Terry, who lived here at Rouse Hill House, near Windsor in New South Wales, until her 90th year. The cedar four-poster bed is early Victorian, the washstand and dressing-table, typically laid out with silver-backed brushes, combs and other toiletries, are mid-Victorian.

Farthest right: Without cornice or dado, this annexe to the bedroom at Meningoort, Victoria, makes clever use of a painted band and modest stencilled decoration to enhance the ceiling. (The same wallpaper was used in the dining-room at Wardlow, page 115.)

A 1903 photograph of a bedroom corner at Rippon Lea, Victoria. Beside the portrait of the owner, Sir Frederick Sargood, are beautiful lace-trimmed blinds, lace curtains and drapes.

WARDROBE
LOUNGE
MANTELPIECE

shall be devoted to increased drawer accommodation. If so, you have your full-length cheval-glass, fitted with candelabra, favourably disposed in another part of the room. Again, you may have the table fitted partly with small drawers, and partly with shelving of polished wood or marble. In our opinion, this piece of furniture ought to be highly ornate in design. A boot and slipper rack should have its fitting locality, and, for the gentleman's purpose, there ought to be a small black enamelled swing shaving-glass mounted on a separate pedestal stand. Perhaps the most prominent article of furniture in the room, next to the bed, will be the wardrobe, the side panels of which might be richly inlaid, and the centre panel filled with a mirror. The chamber should not be without at least one lounge, matching the bed furniture. There should be several easy chairs . . . On the marble mantelpiece should be a tall gold-framed mirror, and in front a pendule of chaste design, with vases and bijouterie . . .[4]

A cynical view is taken by Twopeny in his scant comments on middle-class bedrooms. Bemoaning a general lack of individuality and taste he claims:

The bedrooms are disappointing. Pictures and knick-knacks rarely extend beyond the 'company' precincts. Muttonwool would think it a waste of good bawbees to put pretty things in the bedrooms, where no-one but the family will see them. In these rooms he is au naturel, and with all his good-nature and genuineness he is rather a rough fellow. The brute is expelled from the drawing-room, but he jumps in at the bedroom window.[5]

Twopeny's brief reference to the 'humblest chintz, sheets and blankets' serves to indicate the more basic requirements of the lower-middle classes. The pattern of diminishing quality for persons of lesser rank continues. The mode of decorating bedrooms that were more modest than the principal bedroom of an upper middle-class house varied considerably according to the general degree of ornament of the house's interior. Where the style of the house was generally restrained the bedrooms followed suit, reducing in elaborateness, by degrees, down to the servants' rooms. Although in 'the best bedroom' described by Twopeny 'the bedstead is a tubular half-tester, the toilet ware gold and white, the carpet again tapestry', servant Biddy's bedroom furniture is scant—a palliasse on trestles, a chair, a half-crown looking-glass, an old jug, and a basin.[6]

Sometimes a bedroom of minor significance had no cornice, as such, and was painted rather than papered. A frieze just below the junction of wall and ceiling served as a modest embellishment. In cottages the bedrooms were often treated with pastel-tinted emulsion paint and the ceiling lined with pine boards.

The Kitchen

[The kitchen] has attained at last in our own day the character of a complicated laboratory, surrounded by numerous accessories, especially contrived in respect of disposition, arrangement, and fittings, for the administration of the culinary art in all its professional details . . .[1]

IN DISTINCT CONTRAST TO MOST OTHER ROOMS in the Victorian house, the kitchen was designed to be functional rather than decorative. It was frequently allocated a rather dismal, sunless aspect, while the more socially significant parts of the house enjoyed better situations. Thought of essentially as the 'nether regions', the kitchen area was not within the social bounds of the house except in the humblest of abodes. No self-respecting lady would admit her friends to the kitchen so that the necessity to render it impressive never arose. Consequently, there is very little written in the nineteenth century about the way in which a kitchen should be designed and even less about its decoration. The success of a lady's kitchen lay not in its appearance but in its efficiency and its capacity to produce good meals. No decorative fussiness or frivolity disturbed its businesslike atmosphere.

However, with the effluxion of time and a radical change in life-style in the post-Victorian era, the old kitchen with its primitive decor has come to be seen as attractive in its own right. In particular the earthy textures of the kitchen are appreciated by people of a generation of synthetic materials and bogus treatments. From solid hearty pieces of furniture and substantial fittings emanate a warm down-to-earth quality that appeals widely. Some people find its straightforward composition much more palatable than the sophisticated decorative amalgam of, for instance, the drawing-room.

In contrast to such decorated rooms, the decorative appeal of the kitchen is borne of a naturalness, an uncontrived combination of materials and frugal ornamentation. Whereas in the drawing-room, collections of essentially pretty and non-utilitarian objects constitute the embellishments of the decoration, in the kitchen it is the rows of canisters, the brass and copper utensils, the stack of iron pots, the plates, the scales and the storage jars that enhance the basic furniture. Each of these objects, though marked in the first place for a practical purpose, is also, in a way, worthy of aesthetic appreciation. Harshness of line, crudeness of appearance and sheer plainness were not easily accommodated by the Victorians, even in the kitchen. A dedication to ornamentation and detail shows through, even in the design of highly functional items such as stoves. All these essentially useful and yet carefully designed objects, together with the sturdy wholesome pieces of furniture in an architecturally austere background, gave the kitchen its particular charm.

As a room, the kitchen was both simple and undecorated. It was usually solidly constructed around the chimneybreast and was generally painted a modest off-

white, or a light brown with a darker brown dado or wainscot panelling to dado height. Cornices, skirtings and other trimmings were either absent or minimal. Windows were plain and rectangular, other more stylish contours being reserved for more prestigious parts of the house. Joinery was generally painted in shades of brown, though a drab green was also a possible choice.

Slate or sandstone was favoured for floors in many houses. Some of the more urban middle-class houses had pine covered with linoleum. Others simply had pine boards. Cottages in the country might have had an earthen floor or brick laid on earth. The earthen floor consisted of a special mix of various earthy ingredients including lime, sand, anvil dust, ox blood, cupola ashes, ochre, oil and stale milk. It formed a solid serviceable surface.

The stove in the kitchen is the dominant element. From it emanates the warmth, strength and appetizing smells that give the kitchen a heart and soul. In early Victorian kitchens, the stove or cooking place was huge and open with a combination of iron grids and suspended pots providing the equipment for cooking. By the 1870s cast-iron stoves of many shapes and sizes appeared in profusion. Some had double ovens; some had separate baker's ovens for bread-making. In various forms to suit the size of the kitchen, the cast-iron stove remained standard equipment until well into the twentieth century. According to Twopeny, Australian kitchens lagged rather behind those in England. He states that 'the kitchen is ordinarily very poorly provided with utensils. Ranges and

Above: Typically compact and cosy, this cottage kitchen at Maldon, Victoria, was built in about 1860.

Top left: A Victorian kitchen, built in 1887, with a slate chimneypiece, a cast-iron wood-fire stove, a pine dresser, which was originally varnished, and the original light-fitting. The wall was originally painted dark brown below the dado rail.

Left: The sloping draining-board of kauri pine was a familiar item in Victorian kitchens.

Far left: A section of Victorian wallpaper pasted on to hessian survives in the kitchen of a small cottage near Newstead, Victoria.

The other side of the cottage kitchen at Maldon, Victoria. A steep staircase leads from the door at left to a cellar and storage area.

In a primitive rural dwelling such as this one pictured in the Illustrated Sydney News *in 1873, the kitchen was the complete house, with the bedding and cooking arrangements in the same room.*

stoves are only found in the wealthier houses, the usual apparatus being a colonial oven—a sort of box with fire above and below.' However, judging from the number of stoves imported and produced locally, it seems likely that they were quite common.

In reasonably affluent middle-class houses, the stove was often flanked by a plain but handsome chimneypiece made of slate or heavy pine. On the mantel stood the kitchen clock and other important objects, such as candlesticks and brass-ware. The meat-safe with its wire sides was also an essential piece of equipment in the kitchen.

The other key piece of furniture in the room was the dresser. Used as a repository for all kinds of platters, dishes, cups and bowls, as well as cutlery in the drawers, it was made to be strong and serviceable. Even the smaller ones used in cottages have this quality of strength and simplicity. The standard design has two or more cupboards at the base, with a drawer above each and above this a shelved section for plates which is open. (Glazed doors were added later.) In Australia dressers were made mostly of pine or oak and usually varnished. In large houses there were often two or three dressers in the kitchen and butler's pantry to cope with the quantity of crockery that had to be stored. The bigger plainer ones were in the kitchen itself and the slightly finer ones were in the more elevated domain of the butler. Other significant items of furniture were the table and chairs, which were also usually pine. A bleached scrubbed top was typical for the table. An additional work table or bench was standard in reasonably sized kitchens, some having an inset marble slab for making pastry. A perforated zinc safe for keeping meat and other perishable foodstuffs was also an essential part of kitchen equipment.

A long sloping draining board of thick pine ran towards the sink. Beneath it were pine cupboards, usually with simply moulded doors. Above was often a plate rack constructed of dowelling in a pine frame. In early Victorian kitchens, where the functions of cooking and dish-washing were divided by the use of an adjoining scullery, the kitchen itself was reserved for the preparation of food.

It is difficult to generalize about kitchen light-fittings as they were not governed by precise rules. However, it is possible to say that the basic prerequisite was practicality rather than style. In large kitchens the choice was often a branched one either in brass or iron, not very different from that of a simple billiard-room. Shades were plain, either fluted opaque on a gas fitting, or later the simple 'chinamen's hats'. Before the advent of gas, the kerosene lamp and candles would have been used.

CHAPTER EIGHT

The Bathroom

No house of any pretensions will be devoid of a general Bathroom; and in a large house there must be several of these.[1]

BATHROOMS, AS WE UNDERSTAND THEM, did not appear in the average Victorian house until the twilight of the nineteenth century. Until then, bathing facilities for most people were very simple. Each bedroom was equipped with a washstand and a porcelain toilet-set consisting of jug, bowl, chamber-pot and soap dishes. Waste was taken outdoors and emptied into outside receptacles, drains or cess-pits.

With the introduction of running water to Australian cities, from approximately the 1860s, it became feasible to have a bathroom inside or attached to the house. Melbourne was supplied with running water in 1857. However, the city was connected to sewerage much later. Closets were built outside and were served by the night-cart. From the mid-Victorian period some closets were built indoors, the outer districts acquiring these facilities later. When connection to the sewerage system came, it was possible for a flushing closet to be located within the house. The usual procedure was to put a closet in, or adjoining, the room housing the bath. (From about 1910 this was an accepted formula for the arrangement of toilet facilities.) However, in most simple houses in the nineteenth century the bathroom was still basic and the closet was often separate.

In 1883, Twopeny described the arrangements as follows:

Happily every house has a bath-room, though it is often only a mere shed of wood or galvanized iron put up in the back-yard. In many of the poorer households this shed does double duty as bath-house and wash-house . . . In larger houses, both bath-rooms and wash-houses are much the same as in England. Nearly all families do their washing, and often their ironing also, at home. Of the sanitary arrangements, it is almost impossible to speak too strongly; they are almost invariably objectionable and disgusting.[2]

It was in the more pretentious houses of the wealthy that the concept of the modern bathroom was pioneered. Well ahead of its time was Elizabeth Bay House, with two water-closets in the 1830s. Mansions such as Barwon Park, Mandeville Hall and Labassa and Wiridgil in the Western District of Victoria, Yallum Park in South Australia and Camelot in New South Wales all had their bathrooms close to the bedrooms, in the centre of the house, by 1890. The inclusion of a bath, shower and wash-basin in a room of some comfort and attractiveness was a significant step forward. It was possible for such establishments, especially those in the country, to make their own, sometimes quite complicated, arrangements for the removal of sewage. This meant that water-closets could also be incorporated into the internal facilities at a time when most people were still using a simple out-house arrangement. A range of ingenious flushing mechanisms for pans had been available since the 1850s or

The children's bathroom at Wiridgil, Victoria, includes a bath for small children. Note the typical floor treatment—a wooden lattice over lead.

A typical arrangement of bath and wash-basin with stained and varnished panelled bases and marble tops. Note the bamboo soap-holder and the decorated basin.

Above: The bathroom of Yallum Park, South Australia, displays many of the typical features of middle-class Victorian bathrooms. The bath is set in a solid pine surround, which is panelled and varnished to match the wash-basin cupboard. Panelled timber painted in two shades of blue–green forms the surround for the shower. When the shower was not in use, the three panels folded neatly against the rear wall.

Right: This amazing example from Shanks catalogue, c. 1892, reveals advances made in bath design and embellishments late in the century. The bath may well have found a place in the bathrooms of the upper classes. The suggestion of tiling indicates current fashions.

No. 114ᴬ

This Bath fulfils the sanitary requirements of the age, in that there is an entire absence of wood enclosure, and the possibility of filth collecting behind that enclosure is completely obviated.

The Plunge Bath is of Cast-Iron, with Shanks' Patent Waste and Over-flow arrangement. The Spray may be of Zinc or Copper, with an outer casing of Zinc enclosing all the Pipes, but with a hinged door for access to the Pipes and Fittings at any time. The Shower is of Brass, Nickel-Plated, and the Fittings are Shanks' Patent Eureka Fittings No. 40. The whole thing is perfect and complete in itself. Only three joints are to make, and the Bath is fixed. Great saving in Carpenter and Plumber work is secured.

This Bath is an improved pattern, with Circular Spray like the Eureka Bath, and with the Waste Pipe and Supply Pipes covered in at side of Bath.

PRICE SAME AS No. 114 ON NEXT PAGE.

earlier and were widely used in England by the 1880s. Initially, the water-closet was not part of the bathroom but was placed in an adjoining cubicle. Once sewerage facilities were widely available, fully equipped bathrooms were built in most suburban houses. By the first decade of the twentieth century, water-closets, inside or outside, were the rule rather than the exception in city areas.

The primary factor in bathroom design and decoration was practicability. Surfaces were basically strong and hygienic and could be cleaned easily. Decoration was minimal.

A bathroom lined with wooden panelling, well painted with a liberal supply of varnish in the last coat is good; but the very best lining of all for bathroom walls is real tiling and it is not very expensive.[3]

If you could not afford 'real' tiling, there were varnished papers in imitations of tiles or marble. In the middle-class houses, the walls were generally tiled, at least around the bath area and above the basin. Designs for tiles were not initially very colourful or elaborate, the main type being off-white squares laid in brick style. Often a border of decorative tiles or some other embellishment such as corner spots was found to add a little distinction to the treatment. A fine arrangement remains at Labassa, where ceramic tiles make up the skirting, dado, dado border, filling and frieze.

The bath was usually encased either in pine or cedar and varnished. Frequently a canopy of timber also surrounded the shower end of the bath. The example at Yallum Park shows a folding timber screen that fits neatly back into the rear wall

Above: At Wiridgil, the Manifolds' property in Victoria, this fine-looking main bathroom was built in the 1880s, while two others were provided to serve family and guests. It has the typical panelled and varnished timber surround for the basin and bath. There is a sturdy shower rose with scalloped edge and a folding timber screen to prevent splashing. The bath is zinc-coated and has remained in excellent condition. Three taps marked 'hot', 'cold' and 'bore' provide the water. The marble-topped cedar cupboard and decorative porcelain bowl were a typical arrangement. The wallpaper is not the original.

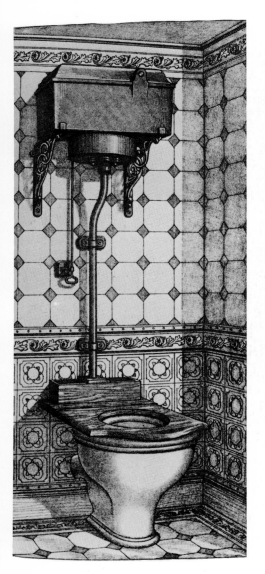

A typical closet illustrated with tiled arrangement of dado, filling and frieze.

when not in use. Lead was used as flashing around the bath. Most baths were of enamelled cast-iron, though an example of a copper bath with zinc coating exists at Wiridgil. It is in good condition and looks impressive in its cedar surround.

The specifications of the architects Twentyman and Askew for a villa residence to be built in Northcote, Melbourne in 1884 include the following instructions:

Provide and fix in bathroom a china lavatory (i.e. wash-basin) of the prime cost value of £2.5.0. to be supported on strong deal frames and to have 1¼" framed, panelled and moulded door in front, hung with brass butts and secured with mahogany cupboard trim for giving access to pipes.

Provide and fix a strong galvanized iron bath, made out of 22 gauge iron, all joints to be chain rivetted . . . The bath to be fitted up with 3" x 2" deal frame and bearers . . . and cap the bath with 1¼" cedar, wrought, framed, shaped and moulded.[4]

It was customary for the plumbing to be much in evidence. The shower and bath taps on the wall were often placed outside the tiles, rather than being bedded discreetly beneath them as is the modern custom. The main taps at the head of the bath were invariably handsome, staunch-looking specimens, made of brass and sometimes zinc-plated.

Basins came in a number of forms. There were porcelain ones in plain white or patterned with flowers matching the pan. Sometimes a semi-spherical porcelain or enamel bowl was made to be set in a timber or marble surround. Cast-iron stands with fitted basins were also available.

Pans of porcelain were somewhat different in design from modern pans and had wooden seats for which they are usually well remembered. Elaborate and lovely floral designs usually adorned both the interior and exterior of pans. Cisterns were made of cast-iron and sometimes were encased in varnished timber.

Colours in bathrooms were generally unspectacular. More importance was attached to the practical aspects of the room than its aesthetics though this did not long remain the case. The usual colour was a shade of cream, buff or light brown for the walls with a buff ceiling. From the 1880s, sanitary wallpapers were made which could be used in bathrooms. As a rule no cornices were used. The only real concession to decoration was a stained-glass window, which served a dual function by retaining privacy for the occupant of the bathroom while providing a degree of natural light. Gas bracket lights were used for artificial light before the introduction of electricity.

Far left: Examples of decorated basins from the Shanks catalogue.

Left: A handsome cast-iron lavatory stand, nowadays called a wash-basin, 'nicely japanned and ornamented', combining 'artistic appearance with cheapness and sanitary value', fitted with Shanks 'Imperial' lavatory.

A conventional arrangement of the late Victorian bath and shower in a suggested setting of decorative tiles.

CHAPTER NINE

Mynda

Kew, Victoria

MYNDA IS A HOUSE OF MODEST DIMENSIONS yet abundant dignity. Having survived without any major alteration, in its original suburban garden setting since it was built in 1882, it has a rare serenity about it. It also bears the mark of an excellent Victorian architect, Lloyd Tayler, who designed it for his newly married daughter and son-in-law, Mr and Mrs M. L. Anderson, as their family home. The Anderson family grew up there and to this day the house is occupied by Miss Elizabeth Anderson, who was the second of the three daughters.

Lloyd Tayler's reputation was earned largely through his design of vast mansions such as Kamesburgh, and public buildings such as the Commonwealth Bank of Australia in Collins Street, Melbourne. In designing Mynda, he exercised his talent for investing a relatively small domestic building with architectural style and distinction. The interior reveals his ability to create a quietly impressive atmosphere, not dependent on opulence for its impact but more on an uncluttered use of architectural forms and a most subtle style of decoration.

While the general layout of the house is conventional, there is, at almost every point and in every detail a clear divergence from the conventional. Each element has a thoughtful individuality about it. The most outstanding example of this is the entrance hall, which, though of modest size, opens into an octagonal vestibule. Rising some six metres, it has a set of eight windows at the top, designed, in the words of Lloyd Tayler, to act as the 'lungs of the house'. Apart from this significant function, the vestibule serves many other purposes both practical and aesthetic. It gives a sense of spaciousness and beauty to the house, it provides access to rooms in four directions and it provides a focal point for the entire house. Its decorative treatment, like its architecture, is simple and yet superbly effective. From the exterior of the house it provides an unusual ornament for an otherwise conventional roofline.

Other notable examples of the distinctive style of Lloyd Tayler are the unusual shapes of the front door panels and surrounds. They are somewhat reminiscent of the Gothic, as are the wooden verandah brackets. Coloured rectangular glass panels in the windows of the drawing-room and dining-room alcoves call on simplicity for their effectiveness, in contrast to the usual highly ornamental glazing effects of Victorian houses.

The absence of complex decorative stained-glass panels and patterned encaustic floor tiles, which were such typical elements of most middle-class houses of the period, serves to reinforce the impression of the individuality of Mynda. Such a house enables us to glean an understanding of the range of styles that were possible in the design of Victorian houses. It shows that within the general bounds of convention there were many ways for variations of style to be expressed, both architecturally and decoratively.

Room by room, Mynda presents a picture of restrained but most effective decoration. Only in the drawing-room does the floral dado filling and frieze

Octagonally shaped, with windows opening at the top, the ochre-coloured vestibule at Mynda, Kew, Victoria, was described by its architect, Lloyd Tayler, as the 'lungs of the house'. Decoratively it is successful, combining an interesting design with the simplest of materials and techniques.

83

Mynda was designed by the distinguished Victorian architect Lloyd Tayler for his daughter and son-in-law, Mr and Mrs M. L. Anderson. Despite its modest size and lack of pretension, or perhaps because of it, he has managed to invest the house with his customary architectural distinction. Mynda was built in 1882.

wallpaper hold sway. In other rooms, their place is taken by a combination of heavily embossed dado papers, used with plain painted surfaces carrying modest stencil designs above the dado and below the cornice. This general formula of painting above the dado is followed in all of the four other main rooms, with some modification in the children's rooms. The colours used throughout are soft and subdued with a bias towards browns and greens. In keeping with the tone of general frugality there are no cornices as such, except in the drawing-room. Beneath the junction of wall and ceiling there is simply a frieze of wallpaper or monochrome stencilled cresting. A look of meagreness is avoided by the use of substantial, rich-looking dados. Their quality sets the tone for the rest of the decoration, making a quietly stylish impact.

The entrance hall at Mynda is bathed in ochre shades. As one enters, shafts of light fall on ochre-coloured walls from lofty windows in the vestibule. Shades of rich brown are repeated in the joinery, dado, frieze and vestibule ceiling. The joinery is painted in two shades of mid-brown, the lighter shade being a little deeper than the 'pumpkin' colour of the walls. The dado is a dark brown, deeply embossed wallpaper, depicting the three levels on which life exists—in the sea, on the earth and in the sky. It shows a marked Japanese influence stylistically. There is a timber rail above the dado, which is a conventional finish for an embossed dado. Above this dado rail there is a band of stencilled work in brown, linking it visually to the wall space. At the top of the wall, just beneath the cornice there is another similar, slightly bolder stencilled cresting executed in the same colour. This rises to a simple rectangular ceiling space in the small entrance hall and to a wooden cornice and panelled and varnished pine dome in the octagonal vestibule. The floor in this area, as in the other rooms, is plain polished narrow hardwood boards (another departure from the usual pine).

The dining-room was originally treated in a manner similar to the hall and vestibule but over the past fifty years has been painted and the ceiling lowered. It is a soft pastel green.

The drawing-room is, decoratively, the most elaborate in the house, though it is by no means an absolutely typical Victorian specimen. It has an unusual shape, taking its access from one side of the octagonal vestibule. In the far corner is an angled alcove of three windows, each with asymmetrically coloured glass panels in the upper third. A further exception to the rule is the dark marble chimneypiece, above which is suspended a dramatic, Japanese-styled overmantel mirror. An exciting contrast is created between the black and gold of the mantel and the light pastel green shades of the wallpaper. There is a conventional arrangement of floral dado filling and frieze wallpapers to decorate the walls. The designs are fully coordinated and employ shades of green, gold and blue in arrangements with a strong Japanese flavour. This effect is more pronounced in the bands of paper that frame the irregularly shaped ceiling. At the corners the bands expand into striking fan-like corner pieces with palm fronds and flowers emphasizing the corner.

Fortunately, several pieces of original furniture have remained in the drawing-room, giving vital clues to its general appearance in former times. The surviving pieces are from the original suite covered in rich red velvet with deep gold panels and braid trim. Curtains in matching shades would probably have hung in the alcove and a carpet square would have covered the centre of floor.

The master bedroom is a simply decorated, spacious room with an adjoining dressing-room treated in the same way. The predominant hue is green, the dado being of heavily embossed, dark green imitation leather paper with rich gold embellishments. Above the timber dado rail of the wall is painted a soft cool green. Below the junction of wall and ceiling is a wallpaper frieze of a floral design in greens and blues. The original suite, consisting of dressing-table, wardrobe and chest of drawers as well as the original half-tester bed, remains in this room. The dressing-room contains the washstand and another chest of drawers. The ceiling of this room carries a modest embellishment of stencilled corner designs, which originally would also have been found on the bedroom ceiling.

The children's nursery is also a spacious, well-ventilated room opening through french doors on to a kind of play-room. The main room has a sturdy dado of pine tongue-and-groove boards painted a soft brown, with a stencilled frieze above the capping. The walls are a soft green, now greatly faded but still bearing their stencilled frieze below the ceiling. The ceiling also has a fine line running some fifteen centimetres from the junction and ceiling and stencilled corner pieces in a soft mid-brown. In general, this room is a most fascinating example of restrained and practical decoration. Although the architecture is straightforward and the detailing modest, the decorative effect is quietly assured and complete. That is to say, all the conventional elements are present but executed in such a refined way as to give a distinctive effect.

While the other rooms of Mynda are important, they do not reveal any of their original decoration as do the main rooms. The great significance of the house as a whole is that it reflects so much the individual and intelligent approach of the architect Lloyd Tayler. It shows Victorian decoration in quite another aspect — that of the unpretentious, softly-hued, simply but distinctively decorated house. That it has survived so beautifully intact to this day is a miracle for which we should all be grateful.

Far right: Part of the original suite of red plush-covered chairs nestles into the corner of the drawing-room of Mynda. Lloyd Tayler's innovative touch can be seen in the glazing style, as well as in the contours of the room, which are emphasized by the ceiling paper. A conventional mid-Victorian combination of dado, filling and frieze wallpapers decorates the wall.

Above: The entrance at Mynda conveys both its modesty as a house and its distinctive charm.

Above right: Departing from the conventional, the drawing-room has a black marble chimneypiece, above which an ebonized mirror hangs suspended, lending a Japanese flavour to the room.

Right: The nursery has the same sense of decorative restraint about it as the other rooms at Mynda. The dado is of simple pine panelling with a monochrome frieze above it. The walls are painted in distemper—a soft green—and carry a modest stencilled frieze below the ceiling. Corner stencils add interest to an otherwise plain ceiling. There is no cornice.

CHAPTER TEN

Mandeville Hall

Toorak, Victoria

St Georges, c. 1860, the home of Alfred Watson. It was later named Mandeville Hall by Joseph Clarke.

Mandeville Hall, the grand residence of Mr and Mrs Joseph Clarke. It was given a new façade and enlarged and restyled between 1876-78 by the eminent architect Charles Webb.

MANDEVILLE HALL, AS A VICTORIAN INTERIOR, was a complete expression of the decorative aspirations of the period. It possessed rooms of quality, taste and grandeur. It marked an unprecedented achievement in domestic architecture and decoration in the colonies and by international standards, it amounted to a coming-of-age. The quality of Mandeville Hall was only ever rivalled by a handful of palatial mansions built around Melbourne in the Victorian period. Many houses were built on as grand or grander scale, but few presented the refined artistry of Mandeville Hall. We have the immense wealth and grandiosity of Joseph Clarke to thank for the opulence of the building, which he transformed in 1876. In more recent years we are indebted to the Sisters of Loreto for their caring custodianship of the largely intact building which forms part of their school.

Built in 1867, the house was at first St Georges and then Athelstane. Joseph Clarke renamed it Mandeville Hall after Norton Mandeville in England, the place from which the Clarkes originally came. Joseph was born in Hobart, Tasmania in 1835, the son of William John Turner Clarke. His elder brother, Sir William Clarke, was created the first baronet of Rupertswood in 1882. Joseph married his cousin Caroline in 1860 and inherited the Tasmanian, New Zealand and South Australian estates when his father died in 1874. He was also elected a director of the Colonial Bank as his father had been. In the same year he moved to Victoria to live.

When Athelstane caught Joseph Clarke's eye it was a simple but impressive twelve-roomed brick house with offices and stabling in Clendon Road. The original owner, Alfred Watson, had died in the previous year and it had passed briefly through the hands of squatter George Hebden, who sold it to Clarke. An early description of the property comments on the fact that a portion of the eight hectares 'was left in its wild state and emus and other Australian fauna were kept there'.[1]

A millionaire, Joseph Clarke paid £12 000 for the property, then lavished upon it all that a man of his standing and wealth could. Major extensions were carried out, increasing the number of rooms to approximately twenty-five. Very much imbued with the aspirations of an English gentleman, Joseph Clarke transformed the house on the grandest scale and used materials of the most exceptional quality. It was said at the time that the house carried 'all the outward appearances of an English gentleman's residence'.[2] The account continues:

The decorations and furnishing are more than usually elaborate, Mr Clarke having gone to the trouble and expense of commissioning Messrs Gillow and Co., of London, to send out artists and workmen specially for the purpose of rendering his new home beautiful to the eye. The interior is decorated and fitted in the early English mediaeval and Oriental styles, and the whole richly ornamented.

The architect for the project was the eminent Charles Webb, who was also responsible for the Windsor Hotel, Scots Church and Parliament Place Terrace

88

(Tasma Terrace). A builder named Harry Lockington carried out the work. The fashionable London firm of Gillow and Company supplied all furniture and joinery from their own workshop. The decorative work was executed by the artist East from England. Consistent with the high calibre of professional men, artists and tradesmen employed on the building was the selection of Sangster and Taylor to landscape the gardens. They had a reputation as the most eminent landscape-designers of their time, both having gained experience in their field before becoming partners.

In all, the works on Mandeville Hall were reported to have cost Clarke £20000.[3] A breath-taking result was achieved by the combination of lavish funds, the owner's aspirations and the professional excellence of those appointed to carry out the work. Accounts of the house after the completion of the extravagant refurbishing are rhapsodic. It was described in *Punch* as having

been decorated not in the shoddy and last-for-a-time manner that we find in a number of our modern houses, but with the utmost skill and the acme of the decorator's art, it may be classed as one of the finest residences in Toorak.[4]

The *Australasian* of 1878 goes much further. It describes the building as

a concert of relevant shapes and colours; . . . a poem of chromatic rhythm and symetric forms, . . . an art-glow whose beauty changes, but does not lessen, with every movement of the eye; . . . a dream, the memory of which comes back with a joyous fitfulness of recollection . . . In truth there is such a flood of beauty that the old allusion of embarras des richesses *almost inevitably occurs to you. You cannot take it all in at once. You are like an imprisoned bee, let loose in a garden of honey-laden flowers.*

The writer gives a vivid picture of the *nouveau riche* stampede for pretentious houses in Melbourne's boom period:

During the last fifteen years, many good houses have been built, some of them worthy to be called mansions, but although a few of these have been decorated and furnished in reasonably good taste, a great many more have not. They have indeed had plenty of money spent upon them, both in the way of painting, papering and furnishing; but although the expenditure has greatly gratified the owner, and perhaps most of his friends, it has often horrified those who possessed either a natural or a cultivated art-taste. And such a waste of money is easily accounted for, seeing that it has been the rule for wealth to be unaccompanied by that sort of education which developes the perception of the truly beautiful.

Noting a recent improvement in this direction he writes:

Our wealthy men have become travelled men. They have seen what money, in alliance with art-knowledge has accomplished in the old country, and there has come into their minds a wish, to spend some of their money in the procurement of habitable houses in the land which is their home.

Mandeville Hall, then, was seen as a significant landmark in the development of taste in the colony. To Joseph Clarke, 'whom everybody knows so well, that it is quite unnecessary, in introducing him, to do more than mention his name', were attributed the esteemed qualities of refinement and worldliness, as well as wealth.[5] It was said that such a house was 'an admirable lesson in taste to those who are privileged to see it and I cannot conceive of anyone living in it being other than refined, gentle and art-cultured. It does credit to Mr Clarke's taste and liberality.'[6]

In the customary Victorian manner Joseph Clarke was judged by his wealth, by the position he held in society and by the grandeur of his house. Praise of his personal and moral worthiness was heaped generously upon him and his family. Sixteen years later the domestic tranquillity and social perfection of his life were rudely shattered when news burst forth of his scandalous association with the scheming and promiscuous Mrs Parker. He was alleged to have given her large sums of money, some £11000 in all, which were invested in various shaky

enterprises, including the Kooweerup Swamp land development scheme. As a result of the scandalous allegations and counter-allegations Clarke's reputation was ruined. He died a year later in 1893.

Moving back to the decoration of the house, the contribution of the artist to the splendid achievement of its interior is acknowledged in the following terms:

it is a monument of which the artist, Mr East may be justly proud. If I were a rich man Mr East would have profitable occupation enough to make it impossible for him ever to wish to leave this colony, and if I were a dictator I would make him director-absolute of decoration both in public and private buildings.[7]

The entrance hall was calculated to have a most stunning impact on the visitor. It is spacious and grand in its proportions and decor. One's eyes are immediately drawn to the lustrous, coffered ceiling with its dazzling overlay of gold leaf. A dash of shiny black surrounds each panel and clear blue edges and margin. Altogether it is a brilliantly bold and rich design. The walls, and particularly the frieze, are equally splendid but in a more sombre, muted way, perfectly complementing the richness of the ceiling.

A solid decorative foundation for the walls is provided by the dado of deep-toned embossed imitation leather paper with its suggestion of classical panels. Rising from the dado border is the main wall design, a superb panoply of large chestnut leaves executed by stencil in a deep olive green on a lighter green background. It is here that one samples the refreshing simplicity of the Aesthetic movement that was emerging in English decorative circles in the 1870s. Nature's intrinsic beauty and strength of design are vaunted in this quiet but arresting design.

Above the relatively loose web of chestnut leaves is the solid, colourful frieze representing the classical saga of Europa and the bull, Diana and other mythological figures. The whole horizontal panorama bestows on the hallway an originality and artistry not often seen in Victorian interiors. It completes the wall surface with a band of rich decoration.

A comparison with a description of this hallway as it was originally is most interesting. Through the eyes of the *Australasian*'s writer we are able to glean much about the attitudes to decoration that prevailed:

The walls were found to be curiously painted of an olive green, so as to imitate the sheen of silk. Then came a dado of stamped Venetian leather in ruby and gold . . . And below this you come to the floor of marble with a real Persian rug, such as sometimes you see in museums; but upon which not often, or perhaps never, you had trodden. And even the panels of the doors were relieved of their flatness by a running leaf pattern in gold, and the furniture of dark oak helped the softly quiet effect of the whole, which softness was still further increased by hangings of rich crimson Utrecht velvet which divided the first entrance from the inner hall.

The suggestion that the walls were painted in imitation of silk strikes one as being a misunderstanding. In a house of such quality the call for imitations would be virtually negligible. A more likely explanation for slight sheen could lie in the use of a protective washable varnish in such a heavy traffic area. More of this contemporary account in the *Australasian* describes with enthusiasm the frieze and ceiling:

Looking upwards, the eye rested upon a ceiling panelled in rich dark brown, black and gold; and as the eye wandered further downwards, it lighted upon a painted frieze which told the story of Europa and the bull, of Diana and Britomante, Meleager, Dictynna, Ersa, Erdymion, Iphegenia and Alphens. These were seen to be pictures painted, not in the hard manner of a mere artificer, but paintings from the hand of a veritable artist, and according to the antique fashion, in use when Apelles wrought such designs, having the name of each figure quaintly attached in the body of the composition.

Off the hallway to the left is the drawing-room and beyond that the

Above: In 1876, part of the highly imaginative concept for the decoration of Mandeville Hall at Toorak, Victoria, was this tiled and stencilled bathroom. A fantastic dado has been created by the painting of underwater scenes on the tiles. Absolutely unconventional, it has a freshness and freedom about it well ahead of its time.

Left: The drawing-room of Mandeville Hall. The furniture and decorations were designed and supplied by Gillows of London. A games table—one piece of the original extensive satinwood suite—stands beside the fireplace, which is also satinwood.

A 1904 picture of Mandeville Hall's entrance, which appeared in Melbourne Punch.

The drawing-room in 1904, when it was the home of Mrs Isabel Ross-Soden and her three sons. The shades of the three chandeliers are facing upwards in this picture, while they were lighted by gas, whereas in the recent picture different shades face downwards for use of electricity. The furniture is a mixture of Victorian and turn-of-the-century pieces.

conservatory. Although the drawing-room has been divested of all but one piece of its original furniture—a small games table—it is nevertheless a room of brilliant richness and beautiful detail. A warm golden glow emanates from the silk damask wall-hanging and is echoed in the rich satin-wood chimneypiece. Swathes of soft light come into the room from the semi-circular bay window and from the conservatory, which was described as 'a large diamond in a rich setting'. Fresh greenery shimmers through the etched glass panels, depicting Pomona and Flora, in the french doors opening into the conservatory. A band of rich red velvet forms the dado in this exceptional room. Above the dado border, which consists of painted moulding, is the main wall-hanging of silk with a motif of branched leaves, possibly olive leaves. Above this is an extremely intricate and delicate tapestry frieze incorporating clusters of stylized fruit and leaves, such as the pomegranate and ivy, in a loose trailing design. The frieze reiterates the rich red of the dado and combines with it the golds of the main wall surface. In this way, the entire wall is brought together by harmonies of colour. The three contrasting textile treatments of velvet, silk and embroidery are combined scintillatingly.

The ceiling is daringly dramatic and geometric. Panels are elaborately decorated in various stencil designs, many in shades of blue and beige with generous gold-leaf embellishments on the margins. In the original furnishing of the room the chairs were covered with this same blue, a turquoise silk, and the window curtains were of the same material. A magnificent camelhair Persian carpet covered the central rectangle of the floor.

In keeping with general practice, the joinery in this room was painted. The colours chosen for skirtings, architraves and doors were two shades of soft green and gold, the lighter shade being used on the receding panels to great effect. The door is further embellished by stylized gold sunflowers in the panels.

Opposite the drawing-room is the dining-room, which must have been the setting for many an impressive dinner in Joseph Clarke's time. Regrettably, we are denied the pleasure of seeing the room in all its furnished splendour. Of the magnificent oak pieces that once filled the room only a suggestion remains: a handsome oak dado surrounds the room and a beautiful chimneypiece provides a focal point. The doorway is immensely solid and tall, expressing the pervasive manliness of the room. This quality is clearly suggested in this account:

Then in the dining-room there is an oak-panelled dado, curiously carven; walls hung with richly-stamped leather, a frieze painted with sporting scenes in the olden days. You will see that the ceiling is panelled in oak and gold, and that the chimney-piece is oaken also, reaching high up towards the ceiling. Above the mantel-shelf there are cupboards and below these there are tiles and brass ornamentation and polished steel and all the suggestiveness of a fine blazing fire and, better still, nothing to remind you of the irritating conventionality of the modern furniture warehouse.[8]

The following description of the room is a graphic insight into the quality of the original furnishings, and also offers a fascinating social slant on the trappings of the wealthy.

And so of the tables, chairs, side-board, and clock. They are of their own kind; solid, and yet of a rare art-work. With the clock especially you will be delighted. It is a tall six feet long clock, such a one for shape as you may many a time, have seen in the farm-houses of the old country. But as this clock of Mr Clarke's cost a hundred and fifty pounds, the resemblance to the farm-house clock ends with the shape. The windows are curtained with costly silk having dadoes and friezes of Utrecht velvet, and the floor is polished and has an Indian carpet in the centre only. There is a feeling of warmth and comfort and habitableness in the room. It does not seem a room only for show for all that everything is so rich and so thorough.[9]

Nostalgic references to the home country seem to reflect Joseph Clarke's own sentiments. Like so many settlers his emotional allegiance was to the land of his forefathers rather than to the land in which his fortune was made and his whole life spent.

The inner hall gives access to the other ground-floor rooms and the staircase. It is an open area largely dominated by a mediaeval frieze bearing the phrase 'Salve-East, West home is best', executed in rich brick red and black. The walls are of a recessive olive-green boldly complemented by the rich ruby tint of the velvet dado and hand-rail. Above the staircase a classic frieze completes the wall-surface decoration. The ceiling is delicately coloured, with stencilled corner pieces.

An enthusiastic description of this area of the house, written in 1878, conveys the grandeur and dignity of the staircase in particular.

The grand stair-case merits its name, but it is not only grand but picturesque. It is broad, and easy of ascent, and all the forms and colours which distinguish it are agreeable and satisfying. In the frieze a good use is made of the classic brick red and black; the walls are of a calm olive green and the dado is of a rich ruby tint. The hand-rail is covered with Utrecht velvet, and on the wall opposite to the hand-rail, there is a rail of brass, parallel to which, upon the wall, there is a band of velvet, as if with the intention of balancing the hand-rail opposite.[10]

A stained-glass window dominates the first landing of the staircase. Executed in strong reds, blues and greens, the central panels depict picturesquely the four seasons in rural England—more evidence of attachment to the home country.

On the top floor the main bedrooms and dressing-rooms occupy the front areas with sweeping views across the garden. The bathroom is centrally placed opposite the head of the stairs. Only the wall surfaces of this remarkable room remain to suggest the watery haven it once used to be. The *Australasian* describes the room as it was originally—a place of fantastic forms and subterranean suggestion.

A recent picture of the stairway showing the ornate newel post, cast-iron balusters and unusual hand-rails. The timber rail has a velvet fringed cover, while the other one is made of brass moulded into a beautiful knot at the end.

A bath hewn out of a solid piece of marble; the walls, lined with tiles, upon which, hand-painted, is a representation of water with mermaids, fishes and swans variously therein engaged. All these creatures are outlined with wonderful vigour and humour. Above this dado of painted tiles, there is the representation of pillars, as if these supported the roof, and between the pillars there are sky, flowers and birds; so that the imagination may readily enough conceive a bath standing by itself in a flower-garden.

The bedrooms also have been partly painted out though the beautiful Adamesque ceilings remain. A description of them indicates their delicacy. It provides an interesting source of information on bedrooms and the prevailing mode of giving each a pastel hue. We can visualize the house in its entirety as it was in 1878, the quality of the main rooms being matched by the luxury of the bedrooms.

Two of the bedrooms are inconceivably luxurious sleeping places, such as houris might repose in. In one, there seems to be a roseate atmosphere; in the other you are conscious of an ethereal effect from the judicious distribution of a blue tint. In both there is an indefinable sensation of softness, smoothness, and absolute repose. The senses cannot help being soothed in such rooms. You would fall asleep and dream of soft music. And the other bedrooms, if less ornate, are all distinguished by an extreme of comfort, and the dressing-rooms are veritable bowers of elegant luxury.[11]

As well as a dazzling array of conventional Victorian rooms, Mandeville Hall could also boast one of the most exotic rooms of the Victorian decorative panorama in Australia. This was an Indian room designed to gratify the prevailing thirst for the extraordinary and the novel.

If a man wished to demonstrate his taste and wide knowledge in architectural terms, it was overwhelmingly tempting to venture further and further into the exotic styles and nowhere more so than in the field of interior design . . . owner and artist alike were off to pursue the exotic, the fantastic and the hybrid.[12]

No doubt Mr Clarke did wish to demonstrate his sophistication and was able to indulge his fancy with his immense wealth and good connections. The Indian

room brought forth rapturous descriptions from contemporaries. Unfortunately the original interior of this room no longer exists, no suitable use having been found for it in a convent. Here is a description of the room as it was originally:

I venture to say there is not another room like it in all Australia. The colours would be startling if they were not in such absolute complementary relation; and the design would seem capricious and over fanciful if it were not so poetically worked out. With the help of a very little imagination, you could easily suppose yourself to be in a temple in a forest. For around you are stone arches, and heavily hanging darkened curtains, while above you is a Persian 'prayer-cloth' upon which are inscribed legends from the Koran. Between the curtains and the silken ceiling, you see sky, and flowers, and birds. The windows seem thus to be almost superfluous. Nevertheless, these are hung with Indian embroidery, and Indian embroidery covers table, chairs and couches and the carpet is Indian also. It seems an inconsistency, in such a room, not to dress in soft flowing Indian garments, and be waited upon by beautiful slaves. Even the gasalier is orientally splendid, being studded with large pearl-like glass balls. On entering this room you unreluctantly sink upon the divan, and fall into a delicious abandonment of aesthetic sensuousness.[13]

The beauty of Mandeville Hall's interior lies in its diversity and its aesthetic cohesion. So much is so strong and rich, yet one is spared the sensation of excess by the careful balance of decorative light and shade, warmth and coolness. Motifs are derived from many sources, mainly classical but also mediaeval and oriental with a delicate smattering of refreshing aestheticism. Joseph Clarke was more than a typical upper-class man of his era; he extended the aspirations of the Australian mansion-builder to exceptional heights by bringing his creation into line with contemporary English trends. He achieved a house that was a vehicle for artistic expression and excellence.

When the *Australasian*'s writer left Mandeville Hall's rooms:

I felt as I have sometimes felt after listening to enthralling music, or after reading a poem . . . or looking at some rare sunset, full of wondrous shapes and harmonious colours; or I could have persuaded myself I had just awoke from a pleasant dream.[14]

CHAPTER ELEVEN

Labassa (formerly Ontario)

Caulfield, Victoria

THREATENED BY SUBURBAN SQUEEZE, Labassa stands like a beautifully adorned woman; her lofty tower maintains a dignified stance while box-like villas press to her skirts. Even so, the spirit of her splendid early years lingers alluringly. The lavishness of her decoration remains resplendent and the European influences in her creation emerge distinctively among her oppressively twentieth-century neighbours. The educated flavour bestowed by German architect J. A. B. Koch can be seen especially in the steep-roofed conical tower, and his interpretation of the general French Renaissance style is evident in the arcaded verandahs on both the ground level and first floor and the balustraded parapet. The façade has a boldness and richness fully echoed in the architecture and decoration of the interior, an aspect that tends to suggest Koch may have had an equal hand in the design of both.

The man for whom this house was built was Alexander W. Robertson, an adventurer from Canada who made his fortune on the Cobb and Co. coaches and on the Mt Morgan mine venture from which he was rumoured to have earned £1000 a week. He is reputed to have instructed his architect in 1889 to build him 'the most magnificent house in Melbourne'. According to the description of the house when it was sold in 1910, his brief was thoroughly executed. It was described as a '*Palatial residence, architecturally perfect and set in beautiful grounds*, of 15 acres . . . the building having been erected REGARDLESS OF COST, inside and outside.'

Unfortunately Robertson did not long remain the proud owner of his dream home, for he died in 1896. The house passed into the hands of J. B. Watson, whose Bendigo mining fortune established him as one of the colony's richest men. The name of the house was changed from Ontario to Labassa, thus erasing Robertson's link with his homeland. After some years in Watson ownership the house was sold by auction in 1910. It thereafter became a boarding house whose many occupants have, over the years, derived much pleasure from the old house. Very recently, in 1980, when the house again came up for sale, the National Trust of Australia (Victoria) bought it with a view to creating Victoria's first museum of the decorative arts, a fitting purpose for a building with so much of its Victorian decoration in evidence.

The interior of Labassa is as original in style and opulent in finish as the exterior. It has been conceived with an eye for expansive spaces and unusual forms. Each room is distinctive and, in its own way, dramatic. Great use has been made of such features as semi-circular bay windows with curved glass panes, internal columns, elaborate chimneypieces, coffered ceilings, remarkable ornamental glass windows and panelled dados. Together with lavish surface treatments and carefully selected themes of colour, the effect of the interior is utterly splendid. The decorative treatment of walls and ceilings relies considerably on sophisticated stencilling, soft colours and the rich textures of embossed wallpapers.

To enter Labassa, one first passes through an entrance archway presided over by two gigantic caryatids. Minton tiles pave the verandah. The front door, painted the original dark green, opens into a wide entrance hall. Each surface is richly treated, the decorative scheme consisting of harmonizing soft greens, apricots and browns and a contrasting splash of brilliant blue–green that appears in the ornamental glass panels above and beside the door and on the stencilled ceiling. A classical atmosphere is suggested by the handsome door-cases and the archway. Parquet flooring, accepted in the Victorian period as the highest quality floor treatment, is used in this and other reception rooms. Heavily gilded embossed wallpapers cover the walls, with a high panelled design giving effect to the dado. Joinery is skilfully toned to harmonize with the predominant colours of walls and ceiling.

The drawing-room/ball-room is panelled in the French rococo manner with a curvaceous painted and gilded chimneypiece playing a dominant role in the stylistic mood of the room. Here the colours are sublimely muted — nothing stronger than a soft green asserts itself. Mainly the colours are cream, blue, grey and apricot used in delicate designs with gold highlights. An adjoining boudoir follows the same decorative theme but with a use of swirling French wallpaper instead of painted walls. The effect is also very rich and refined with a feeling of European elegance not generally achieved in Victorian houses in Australia.

Leading off the entrance hall is another large reception room, possibly used originally as a library. Akin to the hall in style, it makes use of shades of brown and green in a decorative arrangement that includes dado, filling and frieze wallpapers and polychromatic painted joinery. The chimneypiece, rather ahead of its time, is carved oak, stained and varnished.

A group of three rooms on the north-eastern corner of the building presumably housed the dining-room and adjoining billiard-room and smoking-room, though the precise use of each room is unclear. The largest of these three rooms was possibly once the billiard-room. It is one of the most boldly and beautifully coloured rooms one could imagine. From the substantial mahogany door-cases, doors and panelled dado and from the richly embossed wallpaper above the dado emanate a warm brownish ochre glow. A deeply coffered ceiling carries elaborately stencilled ornamentation in the browns and ochres of the walls with the additional touch of a cool deep green. In style the decoration employs

Labassa (formerly Ontario), built at Caulfield, Victoria for A. W. Robertson by the architect Koch.

97

Left: By the most subtle use of colour, the most refreshing design of decorative glass and the richest effects of wallpapering, stencilling and gilding, the architect John A. B. Koch clothed the entrance hall at Labassa, Victoria, in the most flattering attire.

Above: At Labassa, the four seasons provide the theme for the decorative glass panels where the stairway divides. Executed in a striking style, the panels combine red and blue with gold.

Left: The bathroom wall at Labassa is covered entirely with tiles, even to the skirting. A brilliant blue and a clear red against the off-white ground creates crisp bold effect.

Far left: There can be few rooms remaining from the Victorian period with so warm and rich an effect as this one at Labassa. The magnificence of solid timber is coupled with the textural beauty and vibrant colour of the wallpaper, while a superbly stencilled coffered ceiling glows overhead.

Right: Room of mystery, ceiling of mystery. At this stage, it is not known whether this elaborately decorated room was a dining-room, smoking-room or billiard-room. Nor is the precise significance of the painted panels on the ceiling understood. It seems likely that the left-hand one, depicting a ship at sea, marks the birth at sea of A. W. Robertson, the first owner of the house.

Renaissance motifs, the stencilled designs in particular being made up of fine continuous scrolls and floral elements in the Renaissance tradition. Two unusual Corinthian columns, fitted with a band of acanthus leaves just above the dado and a garland of fruit below the capital, stand on either side of a slightly raised alcove area, which has two ornamental windows set in its northern wall. This may originally have been a musicians' gallery or, in the event of the room having been a billiard-room, then it would have been an excellent spectators' gallery.

One other room in this precinct reveals some most interesting original decoration. It is a room with access from the verandah as well as from the adjoining ochre room. Although the original wallpaper was covered with paper this century, the ceiling and cornices are colourful and unusual specimens of Victorian decoration. The key colour in this decoration is a brilliant blue–green while the main motif is the oak leaf. Both elements are repeated in different ways around the room. The cornice contains an oak leaf frieze in vibrant shades of the blue–green. The main wallpaper was also originally of this general design and colour. The vivid blue is linked to the blues and greens of a marine panel painted on one side of the ceiling and to a desert scene on the other. Both scenes are well painted and no doubt were of special significance to Robertson. It was not unusual for men of success to commemorate particularly meaningful episodes in their lives in such a way, incorporating the picture into the decorative scheme of one of their reception rooms. Another example exists at Mintaro, a house in central Victoria which was also the culminating success of the life of its adventurous owner, Robert Gardiner. It is possible that the artist of this work, W. Brettscheider, was also responsible for the work at Labassa.

Labassa is a rarity among Victorian houses. It possesses a wealth of architectural excitement coupled with workmanship and materials of the richest calibre. The six rooms that retain their original decoration provide a marvellous area for the study and enjoyment of Victorian interior decoration. Labassa's position in time, at the height of the boom period, gives it a special significance in the history of architecture and interior design in Australia. Apart from a few stragglers that made their appearance in the early 1890s, the crash of 1892 virtually put an end to the building of houses like Labassa. They were houses where the highest standards of workmanship and the highest quality materials were prized, where impressiveness and quality went hand in hand without reference to cost, to create a gentleman's ideal residence.

CHAPTER TWELVE

Rouse Hill House

Windsor, New South Wales

ROUSE HILL HOUSE HAS THE DISTINCTION, in Australian architecture, of having one of the best-preserved Victorian interiors within a purely Georgian building. It could claim to a number of other impressive distinctions, such as that it is one of the oldest farm properties in Australia to remain in the one family. It is possibly the most beautiful. It is certainly the most pleasing to look upon in the whole country. Mercifully, it has been subjected to minimal change during its long and fascinating history of 160 years. It stands, on a rise outside Windsor, its soft pink symmetrical and shuttered façade facing west, surrounded by magnificent conifers.

The exterior of Rouse Hill House, built in about 1815 for Richard Rouse. Successive generations of the Rouse family and the Terrys have occupied the house until the present day. During the mid-Victorian period its interior decoration greatly altered.

Within its traditional Georgian block it presents a picture of unspoilt Victorian decoration. Compressed into the scale of its Georgian dimensions is the quintessential Victorian interior. Everything that could be considered typical in the way of Victorian decoration, bric-a-brac and furnishings has been included, creating a most miraculous little nineteenth-century decorative microcosm. The techniques of wood-graining, marbling, paper-hanging and stencilling are combined to create rooms of great softness and delicacy. Abundantly, but not excessively decorated, they have charm and an air of tranquillity about them.

The decorative completeness of Rouse Hill makes it one of the most important old houses in the country. It possesses a wealth of information about a whole host of things — how houses were built in the colonial days, how a family lived at such a time, how a house was decorated in the Victorian period and much else. It evokes the ideals, the tastes, the manners and the life-style of a period that is all but lost to us. The Rouse family and their descendents, the Terrys, have successfully kept the house free of twentieth-century contamination. Rouse Hill House is now in the hands of the Commission for the Environment, whose responsibility it is to shepherd it into the last decades of its second century.

The rooms with Victorian decoration and furnishing intact are the entrance hall, the sitting-room, the drawing-room and the dining-room. A fifth room, the school-room, is also of great interest, as are the main bedroom and several other rooms. Each was redecorated and furnished during the mid-Victorian period, all traces of the original Georgian decoration being virtually obliterated. The first stages of this nineteenth-century modernization were carried out by Hannah Rouse, who took several trips abroad between 1869 and 1889, bringing back numerous items for the house. Her daughter-in-law Eliza (Bessie), married in 1874 to Edwin Stephen Rouse, who had inherited Rouse Hill House, was responsible for the completed Victorian interiors that we see today. She and her husband also went on tours of Europe, bringing back additional items for their home.

They accomplished the conversion of the house to the Victorian decorative style within the limitations of its original Georgian dimensions. Fittings such as the original cedar doors and windows remain, complete with their inside shutters,

Right: While the deepest small-paned window reveals the vintage of Rouse Hill House, New South Wales, the imprint of Victorian taste is clear in this corner of the dining-room. Muted floral wallpapers, tinted cornice and family portraits follow the fashion of the mid-Victorian period.

Far right: Faded tawny browns, glowing timbers and lustrous leathers give the dining-room at Rouse Hill House its character. Note the squat Georgian proportions of the room and the corresponding reductions of scale in the Victorian decorative scheme. The furniture was made in the late 1850s by Andrew Lenehan.

Right: Marbled walls, wood-grained joinery, stags' heads and steel engravings typify the Victorian ideal that the owners of Rouse Hill House were following in the 1870s.

Middle right: The internal shutters of the sitting-room of Rouse Hill House are a reminder of bushrangers at the time the house was built. The room reveals the tastes of its occupants of the later Victorian period, especially Bessie Rouse, who began refurnishing the house in the 1870s.

Far right: The drawing-room of Rouse Hill House is one of the most fully preserved Victorian rooms in Australia, even though it is a colonial house. A wealth of decorative minutiae has survived, including drapes on the mirror.

which were once necessary protection against winter cold and lawlessness. But they are now wood-grained or painted, in keeping with the Victorian fashion. These Georgian elements, together with the comparatively low ceilings, give the rooms a unique squatness and air of intimacy. With the reduced height, the decorative formulas of the period are followed, but on a dwarfed scale. The original hand-run cornices have been used without the space-consuming plaster convolutions of most houses. Dados have been used in some rooms but run to a minimum height. Friezes are modest, appearing more like borders. Plaster ceiling roses have been dispensed with, stencilled designs having been used to take their place. The general effect is tinged with modesty and is curiously understated.

The entrance hall is modelled on the English country-house. Clues to this are the splendid trio of stag heads adorning the marbled walls, above the doorways. A rich effect is created by the marbling, which is arranged in large coursed blocks. It is imitative of a yellow marble such as sienna and is carried from above the skirting to the simple beaded cornice. The ceiling is plain off-white. Furnishing is sparse and straightforward. There are a pair of hall chairs and a matching table.

The sitting-room, which one enters to the left of the front door, is of a predominantly green hue. It has a cool, delicate quality emanating from the pretty glade-like wallpaper, which is arranged in the combination of dado, filling and frieze. A green floral arabesque carpet covers the floor. The joinery is painted in two shades of green with a slight contrast of pink. Stencilling, executed also in greens and pinks, is carried around the perimeter of the ceiling most effectively. A curvaceous suite of walnut furniture forms the basis of furnishing for the room. Additional pieces are a davenport and a games table as well as an oval loo table, also in walnut. The chimneypiece in white marble and its gilded overmantel mirror are a typical team. The ornaments are appropriately delicate and white to match the marble. Hanging on the walls are three splendid-looking paintings after Carlo Dolci and Fra Angelico that were brought back from Florence by Hannah Rouse in 1876.

The drawing-room has a similarly reposeful air and is well stocked with walnut furniture and bric-a-brac. It also has a piano and a primitive pianola and other walnut pieces. The surface decoration consists again of pastel-coloured floral wallpapers and a stencilled band around the ceiling. Some parts of the Victorian curtains have survived somewhat miraculously.

The dining-room is imbued with a powerful sense of family tradition. A gathering of fine portraits looks down from the walls. Among them is one of Richard Rouse, who built the house, and his wife, Elizabeth, as well as Edwin and Hannah Rouse, who succeeded them. Warm cedar furniture speaks of family dinners over many decades. The furniture, made in the late 1850s, is attributed to a Sydney cabinet-maker, Andrew Lenehan. A mirror-backed sideboard, laden with silver plate including a huge epergne, sits strong and silent against the wall. As in the other reception rooms, wallpapers of modest quality have been used to decorate the walls. The effect of grained joinery, patterned carpet, leather-covered cedar furniture and muted brown wallpapers is one of comfortable warmth and mellow beauty.

Throughout Rouse Hill House there is a feeling of modesty and a certain intimacy. It is not a robustly assertive house nor a decoratively ambitious one, yet it has dignity borne of its great age and unruffled passage through time.

CHAPTER THIRTEEN

The Acacias

Marryatville, South Australia

THE ACACIAS BLENDS EXTERIOR CHARM with interior splendour. Dr J. M. Gunson built the original section of the house and laid out the gardens in 1877 but it was the succeeding owner, Sir Edwin Smith, who transformed it into a Victorian showplace. He was an important businessman and a member of parliament, as well as being Lord Mayor of Adelaide for a time. He added extensively to the original house, creating a large ball-room with a billiard-room of the same dimensions beneath. Several other rooms were added upstairs to accommodate his family and their visitors. With his considerable wealth and social eminence he made The Acacias one of Adelaide's most prestigious houses, the venue for wonderful balls, parties, picnics and social gatherings.

The decoration of The Acacias matched its excellence as a social venue. A vitality pervades the rooms, many of which are perfectly preserved. Rich wallpapers and superb stencilling are the chief ingredients of the decoration. Colour is used in a particularly scintillating manner. Some rooms are subdued and rich while others, such as the dining-room, are lively and warm. In the entrance hall, beautiful hand-painted panels on the doors and dado ensure that as one enters, the impression of decorative brilliance is conveyed. As in so many houses of the period there is a variety of style and spread of motifs generating a sense of excitement from room to room. The drawing-room is in the traditional Renaissance style, the entrance hall is Japanese in flavour and the dining-room is colourful in a bold Italian Renaissance style. Each room has a distinct identity and evokes a special atmosphere, yet they are bound together effectively by the aura of the house.

It is very much to the credit of the Sisters of Loreto, for whom the house is presently the centre of their boarding-house and convent, that The Acacias remains so nearly intact. It is used, and used fully, by the staff and girls, but the Sisters of Loreto have seen fit not to alter it significantly and to respect its place in history. The magnificent dining-room, once the scene of Sir Edwin Smith's splendid dinners, now accommodates some sixty girls for meals every day. Filled with the babbling of school-girl chatter and cutlery-clatter, the room is alive and vibrant. Apart from the changes in furniture and lighting and the obliteration of the dado, the decoration is as crisp as the day it was executed.

In all, there are now five rooms at The Acacias that retain almost all of their original decoration. They are the entrance hall, the drawing-room and its annexe, the dining-room and the library. There is a strong mark of individuality about each, both in the decorative techniques and in the impact of colour.

The entrance hall captures the most ravishing Japanese effect. Shiny rich colours on the doors, skirting and dado give the room a special glowing quality. The decoration of the dado is especially exotic. Replacing the conventional arrangement of panels and classical designs, is a quite novel, open design of bamboo stems and asymmetrically placed circular panels, each having a different

The Acacias in 1888. The house was the scene of much social activity, including picnics, balls and dinners, especially during Sir Edwin's term as mayor of Adelaide.

The Acacias' splendid owner, Sir Edwin Smith, M.L.C., K.C.M.G., in court regalia.

105

Far left: Sir Edwin Smith's coat of arms sits above the doorway of the dining-room at The Acacias, Marryatville, Adelaide.

Above: The drawing-room at The Acacias follows more conventional decoration, though the grand door surround lifts it above the mundane. There is a band of delicate stencilling on the skirting. Heavily embossed papers create a sense of luxury. A fine piece of angular japonnaiserie exists in the gaselier, and there are also eight bracket lights.

Above left: The powerful influence of Japanese art can be seen in the decoration of the doors and dado in the entrance hall. Freed from the symmetry and repetition of convention, the style is refreshingly individual. Colours contrast dramatically, with splashes of gold on which birds and flowers are painted. Branches of bamboo form the background.

Left: The gallery links the dining-room on the left with the ball-room to the right. The decorative glass panels were executed by Smyrk and Rogers of Melbourne.

107

The gallery, c. 1888. Potted plants are as much part of the decoration as the other elements of the room. Note the way in which the joinery is painted in comparison with the recent photograph on page 107.

The grand ball-room, built as an addition by Smith during the 1880s.

scene, flower or bird painted on its gold ground. To heighten the Japanese effect, each panel overlaps a geometrically patterned circle of the same size. All along the walls and rising with the staircase the effect continues, dramatic and different at every point.

The dining-room is entirely stencilled in an elaborate arrangement of panels around the walls and in a wide bold band ornamenting the ceiling. A sense of roseate warmth emanates from the opulent Renaissance design and rich colouring. The background of the panels is a deep pink. Bands of darker pink, almost a brownish-red, surround the panels and divide them diagonally into diamond panes that carry powderings of a decorative heraldic emblem. The panels are arranged on the soft pastel brown wall colour, each one being surrounded by a fine stencilled design with corner embellishments.

The stencilled work on the ceiling has a free-flowing flamboyance, executed on a grand scale in powerful colours. A strong pink predominates, combined with deep blue, rich brown, dark green and white. The inner margin of the ceiling band is a clear pastel pink, carrying an open simple fret in black that is broken at intervals by a beautiful blue and brown star design. Two superb ceiling roses highlight the centre panel of the ceilings. From them once hung a pair of branched gaseliers, which can be seen in a photograph taken in the 1880s. This photograph also shows the way in which the alcove has been created to accommodate the imposing sideboard and how the stencilled design has been arranged to accent its contours. Such precision and thought characterized the best of Victorian decoration. So little was left to chance.

Leading into the drawing-room annexe, from which guests would make their way before and after dinner, are a pair of most handsome etched-glass doors, set in an elaborate doorway, which carries the Smith coat-of-arms in a focal position above the doors. The doorway is painted in complex combination of soft pastel shades, mainly pink and mauve, with fine highlighting in white, gold, blue and green. The room, though dripping with grandeur, is in no way heavy.

The drawing-room has a more conventional quality about it. An air of delicate richness pervades. The walls are papered in a glistening gold-embossed paper, which has a matching panelled dado and frieze in plaster reliefwork. The general effect is one of mellow greens and golds. There are no strong contrasts of colour

108

but rather the whole scheme consists of threads of related colours and styles woven into gentle harmony. Only a blush of pink on the shades of the gaselier and bracket lights offers a hint of contrast. Possibly the original furniture and drapes would have carried more of this pink. There are some ten bracket lights, which, in this not very large room, gives some idea of their abundance in Victorian times.

Though the room is of a predictable elegant style it is by no means deficient in decorative interest. Above the richly papered walls, the cornice is elaborately coloured in bands of harmonizing browns and creams, which form a perfect frame for the delicately stencilled ceiling. Another special touch is the stencilled band on the skirting. Several colours are used on the upper part of the skirting in much the same manner as a cornice is painted, while the middle panel, which is generally painted a shade lighter than the main colour, carries a charming trailing design of stylized flowers and branches.

The rather imposing doorway and matching chimneypiece bring to the room its only hint of heaviness. Made with lofty mantels and a series of small mirrored shelves on each side, they express much of the later Victorian craving for pretentious display.

A softly coloured, delicately gilded, plaster ceiling rose blends harmoniously into the golds and browns of the room. From it, the five-branch gaselier hangs with arachnid angularity, its central members being made of black china with striking stark designs in white, evidence of the Japanese influence in design.

The drawing-room annexe is, as one might expect, decorated in much the same style as the drawing-room but on a slightly reduced scale. The walls have the same paper dado but with a plain painted surface above carrying stencilled decoration. Both walls and ceiling are of a warm honey colour. A wallpaper frieze of classic style takes the place of the elaborate scrolls in relief in the drawing-room. There is no cornice as such but a band of stencilling and stencilled corner designs give the ceiling sufficient ornamentation.

The other rooms of The Acacias, which are no longer decoratively intact but which can be studied from nineteenth-century photographs, show the magnificence of Sir Edwin Smith's house. The ball-room, and its spacious counterpart, the billiard-room, show the grand scale on which The Acacias was conceived by its grand owner.

The magnificent stencilled dining-room with the table laid for dinner. Note the way the sideboard fits the contours and the stencilling of the alcove in which it is placed. Comparison with the recent photograph shows that only the dado has been painted over since the room was decorated.

Below the ball-room is this rather over-sized billiard-room with its impressive coffered ceiling and unusually tiled light wells.

CHAPTER FOURTEEN

Wardlow

Parkville, Victoria

WARDLOW IS AN EXAMPLE of middle-class decorative ingenuity. It has all the exuberance that characterized the aspiring, appearance-conscious members of the burgeoning middle classes. It was built in 1888, the year of greatest building activity in Australia, by a successful local merchant, John Boyes. He had begun his rise to success as an ironmonger and later prospered in building houses speculatively in Parkville. Wardlow, complete with its fashionable tower, was the most impressive house he built. It is here that the average middle-class style of decoration, middle-class decorative manners and mores can be seen most clearly. Here is the typical style of the average shop-keeper, merchant, professional man or government official of the time. Allowing for variations of scale, it is the same general style of terrace houses, villas and the average 'gentleman's residence'. On a more modest scale, it is the style of cottages and small houses. It is the most widespread style—suited to those who were making a comfortable living but who were not wealthy. It was the style for those concerned to improve their circumstances for a moderate expenditure, without straining themselves in the direction of individuality.

At Wardlow all the decorative resourcefulness of the period is to the fore. Every decorative device, whether genuine or false, from wallpapering to wood-graining, is pressed into service. All surfaces carry elaborate designs, often in a multiplicity of colours and patterns. Decorative coyness has no place. Instead a zesty extrovertedness can be discerned in every aspect of the decoration. Pleasure and confidence in the good-looking products of industry show themselves in the architecture as well as in the furnishing and decoration. Cement ornaments, cast-iron work and decorative tiles enhance the exterior, just as plaster mouldings and other fittings form the basic decorative framework of the interior. Within the house, wallpapers especially abound. Not just the conventional dado, filling and frieze but extra bands and borders are used in conjunction with painted bands in the cornice and on the ceiling. Flowers of all kinds are profuse. Ceiling papers of geometric design occupy the main ceiling areas. Joinery is either wood-grained and over-stencilled or painted in tones complementing the wallpaper.

For all its energetic decoration, the effect of Wardlow is full of repose. Despite a myriad of patterns there is no conflict and no harshness. The colours are carefully harmonized and the patterns skilfully blended into cohesive decorative entities. Each room has a predominant colour that establishes its individual tone—whether it is light and elegant as is the drawing-room or slightly brown and rich as is the dining-room or greenly sombre as is the parlour. Each has a theme of decoration that is carried through the room so that wallpapers and furnishings are coordinated. Each room has a distinctive aura of its own.

The four rooms that remain substantially intact at Wardlow are the entrance hall, the dining-room, the drawing-room and the parlour. The entrance hall has a rich shiny brown feeling about it. Both the joinery and the wallpaper contribute

All the trimmings of the typical middle-class entrance hall can be seen at Wardlow, Victoria. Dado, filling and frieze wallpapers are varnished for serviceability. Colourful decorative glass and the lantern light-fitting add sparkle to the room, and a crisply patterned encaustic tile floor is both practical and decorative.

111

The splendours of wood-graining were much relished by the average Victorian home-owner.

Wood-graining again enhances the simple pine door to which it is applied. Note the typical arrangement of door furniture.

to this effect. The dado paper is divided into alternating panels of classical style. Above it there is a border from which rises the open floral design of the filling. The frieze continues the floral theme though in a more horizontal manner. The entire wall is varnished to give a durable washable surface and also to create a certain glossy decorative effect. The joinery is wood-grained in yellowish tones of oak and maple. The tiled floor offers a lively element of pattern that prevents the decorative scheme from sinking into gloom. The ceiling, which is surrounded by floral bands and a colourful cornice, gives added interest to the room. The final splash of beautiful contrast is provided by the stained glass surrounding the front door and in the typical hall lantern. The general decorative success of the room is achieved by the effect of the sparkling contrasts in glass and tiles and cornice highlights against a sombre wall treatment.

The drawing-room has particular charm and elegance. In colouring, it is predominantly cream and gold, the wallpaper consisting of large motifs, in the French style, against a cream ground with a matching crested frieze. There is no dado. The cornice is relatively light and simply coloured in cream and beige. The ceiling has a softly coloured margin of painted decoration depicting flowers and arabesques. In the centre is a gold and cream painted ceiling rose surrounded by a mild geometric paper. Rich and elaborately tasselled drapes hang in the window-opening. Made of greenish-gold silk damask, with brown velvet trims, they are remarkable survivors of an extinct style of draping. Originally, lace curtains would have hung against the windows. The joinery is wood-grained in imitation of walnut, with an added embellishment in the door panels of stencilled work in gold and black. Its effect is rich and yet delicate, an interesting example of combined techniques. Typically, the chimneypiece is white marble and the tiered wooden overmantel is bedecked with vases, statuettes and other ornaments.

The furnishing is of French origin, as is the wallpaper. The style is an adaptation of what Rocke would have called 'Parisien'. It has a typical suite consisting of seven pieces—settee, lady's and gentleman's chairs and four single chairs—the pieces being light and fine. They would originally have had damask covers with velvet trimming and corded edges. A few tables, a whatnot and a canterbury complete the furnishing, apart from a collection of gold-framed paintings hung on long wires from the brass picture-rail in the characteristic angled manner. Unfortunately, the original carpet square and the light fitting have been replaced.

The dining-room has a fullness about it. Far from the sobriety of many Victorian dining-rooms, this one is flowery and full of pattern. The key element is, once again, wallpaper, which is used with splendid vigour. It follows the conventional pattern of dado, filling and frieze with a bonus of several floral bands in the cornice and leading on to the ceiling. If ever there was a room that could be described as 'typically Victorian' this surely must be it. There is such an abundance of decoration and yet it is all worked into a quite striking and cohesive whole. A subtle shade of brownish pink predominates in the room. The marble chimneypiece is this colour and the wallpaper and joinery have been chosen to follow this theme. Shades of apricot, grey, brown and pink are brought into play most sensitively. Judicious contrasts are provided by the use of green and other cooling colours in the cornice and by the cunningly dramatic choice of black to accompany the brownish pink on the joinery. Another diversion from the warm browns is in the green and gold treatment of the ceiling rose. A delicate star design of wallpaper covers the ceiling.

The dining-room has the typical late Victorian suite of furniture consisting of table, eight chairs, sideboard, chaise-longue and dinner-wagon, all of which carry decorative motifs that match the overmantel. Several handsome oil-paintings decorate the walls, completing the effect of richness and decorative fullness so enjoyed by middle-class Victorians.

A more contemplative room at Wardlow is the little parlour, which may

originally have housed bookshelves and a round table as well as the horsehair covered easy chairs that are there today. Again it is entirely wallpapered, though with some degree of restraint compared to the dining-room. The key colour of the room is green, which appears dominant in the small-patterned floral wallpaper. A minor novelty to the decorative scheme is provided by the band of wallpaper running along inside the concave section of the cornice. Stencilling was sometimes used in such a position also, usually in grander houses. A small floral paper runs, in a busy fashion, over the ceiling.

The marble chimneypiece is, in this case, a sombre grey, in keeping with the general tone of the room. It has a cosy comfy air, entirely in the spirit of the house generally. Wardlow is devoid of intellectual gravity but abounds in decorative flair and exuberance. Above all, it is a most important example of the decorative style which, with variations, would have characterized the majority of middle-class Victorian houses in Australia.

An 1890 photograph of Wardlow, the Parkville home of John Boyes, indicates the fashions of exterior decoration, as well as giving a glimpse of the practices of interior window treatment. The house was built in 1888 and is typical of many houses built at that time of economic expansion.

Right: An awareness of colour sympathies emerges clearly in this comfortable corner of Wardlow's dining-room. Every element is somehow absorbed into the theme of colour, dictated by the pinkish brown chimneypiece. Apricot, pink, grey, brown and black blend and harmonize.

Above: The talent the Victorians had for combining patterns can be seen in this play of designs and colours from the dining-room into the entrance hall of Wardlow.

Right: Wardlow's drawing-room with original drapes, wallpaper and suite of furniture (with modern covers).

Far right: With a total addiction to a fullness of decoration, Wardlow's dining-room combines wallpapers with a number of narrow bands of paper augmenting the decorative impact of the cornice. A striking choice of colours enhances the joinery.

CHAPTER FIFTEEN

An Approach to Restoration

A minor bedroom at Glenleigh, New South Wales, where restoration has reinstated original colour-schemes and stencilled decoration.

SO OFTEN ONE READS ALLURING DESCRIPTIONS of houses which purport to be restored. So often all that they describe is a house that has been made shipshape and that is vaguely Victorian. As a general rule the house depicted has been radically transformed and its interior will have had its Victorian decorative character ruined. It may mean that the house has had some of the Victorian elements such as the fireplaces, decorative glass, plaster mouldings or doors replaced or very nicely repaired. The whole house may be painted, papered, carpeted and generally refurbished. But this is hardly restoration.

For practical purposes where work follows the original but involves some *minor* degree of new work or material, then it may be termed restoration. Where the work is substantially new, then it can no longer be called restoration. For instance, if a ceiling rose has a fragment missing but is otherwise intact and painted in its original colours, then to mould another fragment and paint it to match would come within the broad compass of restoration. However, if the ceiling rose is missing altogether, to find another one and put it up and paint it in the Victorian manner would not be restoration, it would be reconstruction. In effect this would be building a new ceiling rose, one not related except in appearance, to the original one. To go a little further, if the ceiling rose is missing and there is no definite evidence to suggest there ever was one, then to put one up would be a hypothetical construction; it would be actually recreating a broadly appropriate element without it having any known relevance to the original. Once one begins to depart from the known qualities of the original, then the work ceases to be restoration or reconstruction. Once compromises or adaptations are made, the work can only be described as recreation or renovation. Restoration should be done scrupulously well and with the greatest sensitivity and accuracy.

This leads to the question of what should be restored, recreated, reconstructed or renovated in a house. Lack of understanding and sympathy for Victorian houses, particularly in the past twenty years, has resulted in some brutish treatments of houses, carried out in the name of improvements. Architecturally ruthless people and opportunists have massacred battalions of Victorian houses and left only a handful of innocent survivors intact. It is time we took stock of the rapidly diminishing resources of our Victorian houses. It is also time we did something to respect the integrity and character of those that survive. For those severely mutilated, a course of sympathetic handling and imaginative construction may be the only answer.

A three-tiered set of proposals which, broadly, aim towards reversing the downward spiral in the treatment of Victorian interiors could be implemented.

1. First, original decoration should be restored wherever possible. Sometimes the resources required to achieve this may be considerable. In other cases it may be just a question of establishing original decoration as a high enough priority and taking appropriate measures to accommodate it. Sometimes the kind of effort required is sheer, painstaking toil. Whichever way it is achieved, by a combination

of resources or an effort in a certain direction, the result will almost certainly be worthwhile. Original elements in an old house invariably lend depth, character and individuality. Each fragment that is original, even a patch of old wallpaper in a cupboard, a wood-grained door, or the tiles in a hearth should be regarded as precious. They are the tenuous threads by which we can reach back into the past. It is far better to be *very* conservative about *any* original work, no matter how unprepossessing it may look or how dilapidated. Many a would-be restorer has destroyed most important and interesting material in a burst of zealous cleaning-up and redecorating that he has subsequently regretted. At the very least, if there seems no reasonable way of retaining all of an area of original work, then retain one section, for instance a part of a wall with original wallpaper on it. Far from marring the overall effect of the room, it will enhance its interest.

An upstairs bedroom at Woolmers, Tasmania, recreated in the early Victorian style.

Wallpaper that has come away from the wall can be glued back again and old missing patches painted in on the lining paper; stencilling can be lightly touched up or the design traced, a new stencil made and any missing parts reapplied; wood-graining and marbling can be touched up very easily, as indeed they were made to be. Broken tiles and other breakable items can often be glued together again just as one repairs furniture. Surely it is better to mend the broken leg of a chair than to throw the chair away? So it should be with decoration in a room; everything possible should be done to retain any original elements. The chapters on wallpapers, stencilling, wood-graining and marbling should be of assistance.

2. If there is evidence of any of the original decorative treatments of a room, then those treatments should be reinstated or reconstructed as closely as possible to the original. For instance, if the joinery has been wood-grained originally then it is desirable to wood-grain in the same manner as it was first done. If the walls were originally papered, then they should be papered again in the same style, or as close to it as possible. Similarly, any stencilled work should be reinstated just as it was originally. Many people would argue with the desirability of this approach. My reason for advocating it is simply that I believe that the way a building was decorated originally is the most satisfying way for *that* building to be treated. Adhering to the original style of the house both inside and out is the only way in which that particular house can retain or regain its integrity. Any styles or values that one may prefer are impositions on the basic character of the house. The greater the magnitude of those impositions, the less the spirit of the house can express itself. The more one can interpret the spirit of the house and augment its decorative expression, the more complete will be its integrity. It is this integrity to me which is all-important, not what appeals to this or that person, but what *belongs* to that house. The most modest or the most garish of houses achieves some beauty and distinction if it can just be itself. Once it becomes the vehicle for modern taste it rapidly begins to lose its own dignity. The greater the interference with the structure and surface decoration, the greater the loss.

A union banner of 1910 shows the techniques involved in the decoration of elaborate rooms in the Victorian period.

A house that is overshadowed by transient personal whims is more like a shell of a house—it has ceased to express its own identity and conveys a message of confusion. Harsh, jarring notes frequently mar the tranquillity. Beneath the scars of alterations, extensions and conversions, such houses cry out for sensitivity and respect. Unless personal taste is in sympathy with the original fabric of the house, then it merely sits uncomfortably on it. The most successful houses of any period are surely those in which the personality of the owner and the house go hand in hand. When the owner respects the individuality of the house and does not try to bend it towards another end, then a sweet harmony ensues. Therefore, the ultimate goal is to recreate an interior that belongs to the house, which enables the house itself to speak.

Victorian houses were designed to wear certain kinds of decorative clothes, and the trimming and restyling to which they are so often subjected nowadays are generally unflattering. This is not to deny that many beautiful and practical effects can be achieved in remodelling Victorian houses but they detract from the

Above: The entrance hall at Oxford, Victoria.

Above right: The bathroom at Oxford. The bath, tiles and decorative glass window in this room are original.

Right: In 1978 the National Trust of Australia (Victoria) re-created a Victorian interior in its headquarters at Tasma, Parliament Place, Melbourne.

Far right: Painstaking restoration and reinstatement of paint and stencilwork above the tiled dado and on the joinery at The Abbey, Sydney, has revealed work of great beauty, originally executed in 1881 by Lyon and Cottier of Melbourne and Sydney.

fundamental integrity of the house. The charm of the original decorative scheme is that it reflects the combined aspirations of the original owner, architect, builder, tradesmen and decorators, which, in totality, reveal the essence of the house as it was first conceived. Other conceptions may follow but none has the validity of the first. Others may be more pleasing aesthetically but none can match the first for appropriateness and genuineness.

There are many factors governing a building today. In particular, its use may vary greatly from its original purpose. Churches become houses, warehouses become theatres, houses become offices, mansions become museums. One cannot be too dogmatic. However, the further a building strays from its original setting, structure, appearance and decoration, the greater the risk of its debasement. Only in the hands of the most sensitive persons can radical transformations leave the spirit of a building intact. There are thousands of houses that are a mish-mash of elements, a pot-pourri of inchoate ideas. The real gems are those that have survived, from any origins, with an untrammelled spirit and a distinctive cohesiveness. They are little capsules of human aspiration and achievement.

Within the appropriate stylistic context of a house, there is abundant scope for individual personality to express itself. The selection of harmonious decorative elements and the arrangement of the contents of a house to achieve a cohesive result are the great pleasures of a Victorian house. Without personal touches of flowers, paintings, ornaments, plants and general garnishing, a room cannot come to life. The joy of it all is in seeing a Victorian house revivified, singing its own tune in a new age.

3. Where there is no particular evidence or knowledge of the original decoration, then broadly appropriate sympathetic Victorian decorative treatments should be selected. This is largely a matter of choice but I prefer decoration that relates in style to a house rather than something that is stylistically different. Victorian treatments for Victorian houses make more sense to me than any other alternative. Modern Mediterranean, contemporary Australian, Swedish traditional, rustic colonial, and other favoured styles suggest painful incongruities. A sympathetic approach is surely better.

Comparison of identical buildings, such as those in a row of terraces, which have been subjected to sympathetic and unsympathetic treatments can be revealing. An opportunity to make such a comparison exists at the offices of the National Trust of Australia (Victoria) at Tasma Terrace, Parliament Place, Melbourne. Parts of the terrace, numbers 2, 4 and 6, have been decorated with polychromatic colour-schemes. Numbers 2 and 4 have rooms that have been carefully constructed and furnished in the spirit of their original decoration. The others, numbers 8, 10 and 12, are treated in simple stark one-colour schemes. The severity, especially of the all-white scheme in 12, kills the spirit of the rooms.

In the absence of any original Victorian decoration, it is best to adopt the same approach to the decoration of a room that the Victorians would have followed. Before proceeding with details of that approach, I would like to make a few generalized remarks as guidelines about decoration. It is important to understand the thought-processes behind Victorian decoration in order to appreciate it and to restore or recreate it.

For the Victorians, decoration was a serious matter, not something arrived at haphazardly. Decorations were not merely competing elements swamped by mindless clutter. The Victorians admired complexities of pattern and subtleties of colour and revelled in their skilful, harmonious combination. They established a decorative style that was distinctive for its abundance of ornament and richness. A fundamental belief that plainness and 'crude utility' were to be avoided, led them to apply decoration, by our standards, very generously. Walls and ceilings were decorated in a coordinated scheme, the colours of the walls being echoed on the ceiling. Blatant, harsh contrasts of colour were abhored, while harmonious combinations were the ideal. Primary colours were used rarely and then very sparingly, usually to give a highlight to a complex decorative panel. White also was not generally favoured in decoration until the 1890s, when it began to be used in combination with pastel colours. Preferred colours during the 1870s and 1880s were the tertiary blends of greens, browns, reds, blues, pinks and golds. Great care was taken to soften each colour by the admixture of a little of another colour. In the painting of joinery these shades of a colour were important in highlighting the theme of colour on which the decoration of a room was based.

Also very important to the Victorians was establishing the relative importance of a particular room. The hierarchy of decoration dictated that the most elaborate decoration was applied to the front rooms of a house. Towards the rear, the schemes were simplified just as mantelpieces and plasterwork became more modest. It is important to recognize the original style and status of a room, and to redecorate it accordingly, not over-treating modest rooms and not starving grander rooms of their former riches. Careful investigation of all elements in a room is the best way to build up a picture of the room.

In endeavouring to restore a house or to redecorate it in an authentic manner, it is necessary to understand what the Victorian occupant of the house was striving to achieve. Ideally, one should immerse oneself in the character of the house and learn as much as possible about the techniques employed in its decoration. In devising a decorative scheme for a particular room, one must first take stock of the architectural elements. Doors, windows, archways, fireplaces, cornices and ceiling roses are the skeletal elements around which the decoration will be arranged. One should determine the general style and spirit of the room in decorative terms. Should it be stencilled and wallpapered in combination or mainly consist of one or the other? Should it have a dado? If so what height? What should be the predominant colour theme? Sketch out your ideas on paper. Try to visualize the whole effect. Establish key elements such as wallpapers or stencil designs and then work the rest of the scheme in around them. Bearing in mind that the range of appropriate wallpapers including borders and friezes is not as great as it should be and that other items such as picture rails or dado rails may have to be sought out, be prepared to take time and trouble to piece the scheme together. Every portion of the polychromatic decoration should be devised and disposed with the view of accentuating and enriching the architecture. The individual elements require some explanation and advice on their decoration.

Dado

The historical precedent for the use of the dado was the interior decoration of the houses of Pompeiians. Their decoration of the wall in three sections with the dado at the base enjoyed a spirited revival during the Victorian period, reaching its zenith just before the turn of the century. The dado's use began early in the century, some pre-1830 examples existing in Australia. Its purpose was twofold. First, it was designed to withstand wear and tear. A strong wallpaper dado or deeply coloured oil-painted dado could well withstand the knocks and scrapes of hallways, staircases and kitchens. The dado's other function was as a decorative feature. It was intended to 'break up the monotony of the surface mass.'[1] It offers opportunity to introduce contrasting colour-texture and design, which is a very important consideration in relation to Victorian rooms with their high ceilings. To omit a dado from the decoration of a room where one formerly existed, causes the wall to become excessively blank and boring. The dado also conveys 'a snug, "closed-in" sentiment'. The room is, in effect, embraced by the dado. Its other powerful function is to provide a base for the decoration of the wall. In its many forms it is designed to appear more solid and dominant than the wall above it. The suggestion of masonry and the use of geometric forms in close arrangement give this effect of creating a visual foundation on which the rest of the wall is based.

The height of the dado varies in different houses from approximately a metre to

The stencil cut by the restorers Elizabeth Stevens and Chris Crooke for their work on the entrance of The Abbey, Sydney. The design was cut out of stencil paper and paint applied with a small roller.

DOORS

Wood-graining and floral ornament make a colourful splash on this late Victorian door.

A door, simply painted to blend with the wallpaper in the drawing-room, at Merigal in New South Wales.

A drawing-room door, painted and delicately stencilled, at Mynda, Victoria.

CORNICES

A fine array of colours adorns the cornice and ceiling of Yallum Park, South Australia.

The ceiling colour in the billiard-room at Eynesbury, at Melton, Victoria, has been chosen to echo the soft blue in the swirling floral wallpaper of 1885.

CEILING ROSES, CLOCKWISE STARTING AT TOP LEFT

Cherubic figures revolve around the ceiling rose in a terrace house in Fitzroy, Melbourne.

Shaded leaves, berries and buds give a soft natural effect to a library ceiling rose.

Glistening with green and golds, this ceiling rose is in a dining-room.

A typical ceiling rose, in the dining-room of Westella.

Gorgeous grapes and posies of flowers in pastel shades make this ceiling rose a novelty.

Soft shades of cream and beige, give this ceiling rose its depth and richness.

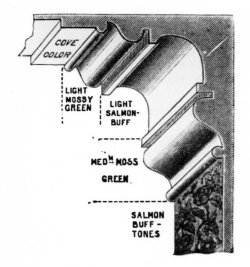

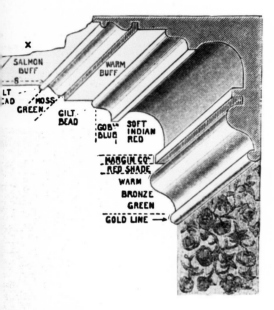

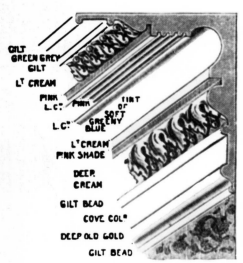

The painting of cornices.

a metre and a half. It should never reach above the mantelpiece unless the material used is wood-panelling. Generally it comes close to the mantelpiece and is capped by a timber rail, wallpaper or stencilled border.

The materials adapted to dado purposes are innumerable. Firstly, there is simple oil-paint, which, used in the most practical areas, has a line of dark brown or black above it. Then there are the possibilities of American oilcloth (like linoleum), Indian matting, cretonnes, twills, brown paper (which can be finished with painted decoration), plain 'oil-grounded' papers, Lincrusta Walton, Willesden paper, Tectorium (thin textile covered with painted patterns), leather papers, Alabastine, Anaglypta, and in the luxury class, velvet. The dado was a part of the decorative scheme that was considered important enough for a variety of materials of all classes.

Cornice

Cornices and ceiling roses are another part of the decorative scheme that calls for particular knowledge. They were frequently linked in style and colour and the approach to colouring them is similar. However, I will concentrate particularly on cornices as they present a challenge to the decorator. They also have a most significant contribution to make to the decorative impact of a room. The Victorians paid considerable attention to the technique of painting cornices. 'To leave the cornice white, or even the same tint as the ceiling, looks altogether weak and poor'.[2]

The general idea of painting the cornice was to 'tint' it to match the wall colour. The complexity of this tinting varied considerably according to the elaborateness of the general scheme. It may mean that the whole cornice was tinted one colour or that it had a few beads or lines of additional colour. Or it may be that the cornice was coloured with many and various colours to contrast with or harmonize with the wall or ceiling decoration.

In all cases, the purpose of the cornice is that it should, in its entirety, frame the ceiling. If several colours are used, the darkest colour should be at the base and the colours should lighten up to the ceiling. The deepest tones should always be darker than the general wall colour. Gilding should be applied to the advanced portions that catch the light. Make up the various amounts of colour in separate pots; then put a little red into green, green into red, and so on, until they are sufficiently soft and neutralized to give a restful and harmonious effect, unless you begin with colours that are already suitably soft. Try the colours on a section of the cornice, testing their effect on each other and on the room generally. Above all, look at examples of original coloured cornices whenever possible and try to incorporate the sense of colour they impart to your work.

Ceiling rose

The ceiling rose was often a room's most splendid decorative element. Their colouring and shape were frequently rich and dramatic. (Yallum Park's billiard-room rose is a stunning specimen.) The technique of their painting varies considerably from house to house, some having an abundance of gilding and lavish colours while others are quite modest. In all cases, the basic colour relates to the wall colour and should be applied first. The next step is to highlight the advanced portions with appropriate colours. The variety illustrated should assist. Finally, gilding is applied to the most significant parts.

It should be noted that in Australia plaster ceiling roses were highly favoured and appear in the majority of middle-class houses. However, stencilled roses were also used, sometimes in more modest circumstances and always in conjunction with stencilled decoration around the ceiling. Old Government House, Sydney, was found to have stencilled roses in its original decoration. It is often difficult to find such decoration as it has usually been over-painted. Only by shining a torch across the surface of the ceiling does the raised outline of stencilled work sometimes show. Careful scraping and paint removal can reveal the design.

Frieze

The frieze formed a most significant part of wall decoration. Running in a horizontal band, it formed a contrast to the main wall section below. To reinstate a frieze, there is a basic decision to be made between the choice of wallpaper or stencilled work. If the room is to be predominantly wallpapered, i.e. if the main part of the wall is papered, then the frieze should be papered with a complementary design in harmonizing colours. If the main part of the wall is painted, there is rather more scope in the choice of a frieze. A wallpaper frieze of appropriate colouring could be found or a stencil design devised. Any frieze does much to enhance a Victorian room, as it embellishes a visually significant part of the room, the space below the cornice. It also helps to break up the vastness of the wall space, which is so much part of the decorative concept for Victorian rooms.

Ceiling

The ceiling takes its decorative cues from the rest of the room. According to whether the room is predominantly wallpapered or painted, the ceiling is treated similarly. If it is to be papered, the choice of designs is reasonably wide. Provided the colouring is a pastel shade harmonizing with the wall colour, the only other factor is that it should not have 'a direction' in its design. In other words, it cannot be seen to flow either lengthwise or sideways. It must be the same viewed from any direction. For this reason, any geometric design is ideal, either dots, stars, circles or interlocking geometric motifs. In the Victorian period the most popular were the lustre papers, which had soft, self-tinted designs with a silvery lustre. If the ceiling is to be stencilled in keeping with the rest of the room, or as was commonly done, in contrast to a wallpapered wall, then corner designs can be selected. (See Chapter 18 for examples.)

The other aspect of decoration that has not been specifically covered is that of colour. The examples provided of original decoration convey much of the Victorians' technique for the use of colour. A brief analysis of the qualities of colour follows.

Victorian colours

While it must be understood that there are no absolutes as far as colour is concerned in Victorian decoration, the following general comments are offered as a guide to colour choice.

Green. Although green is not a primary colour, in its brightest shades it is too assertive, and accordingly calls for skill and taste in its use. As a rule, bright green (i.e. grass green) is inadmissable in painted decoration. The greens used should be mixed with other colours, such as brown, red, ochre, orange and purple, to suit the purpose of its use. Many useful tints can be so formed from green, which contrasts more agreeably with all colours than any other individual colour.

Blue. Blue is a most retiring colour, possessing a quality of coldness. However, if carefully tinted with green, producing a soft duck-egg blue and other similar shades, it can be useful. Stronger blues can be used at a greater distance in small amounts to good effect. Blue can also be used for decorative purposes when mixed with black to form the slate-blue range of colours.

Red. Red is the most positive of all colours, imparting warmth to the colours with which it is mixed. It is a potent element in harmonizing other colours, and in reconciling such discordant colours as blue and green. Pure reds are seldom used, and then only sparingly. Crimson–reds are useful as a ground for gold. However,

Fig. 1—Diagrams of side of Pompeiian House, after Owen Jones. Fig. 2—Wood dados: three simple panel treatments, A, B, C. Fig. 3— Anaglypta dado. Fig. 4—Anaglypta dado in a diaper design. Fig. 5—India matting with bamboo dado rail. Fig. 6—Lincrusta: imitation carved wood.

This small miner's cottage, c. 1885, at Green Gully Creek near Castlemaine, Victoria, has the original paintwork on the joinery and varnished cedar chimneypiece and pine ceiling. The walls have been repainted recently in a modern equivalent of the original blue, which was found under layers of wallpaper. Many country houses were painted with cheaper distemper paints instead of being wallpapered.

the most useful and harmonious reds are those known as etruscan, terracotta and brick reds, in which browns and tawny yellow enter largely.

Yellow.   Pure yellow should be used sparingly. The other yellows formed by combination with browns, the ochres and siennas, form a choice family of colours for decoration. Mixture with green is also very successful. A range of buffs can be made by mixing white with the yellow–brown combination.

Brown.   All yellow–browns are of great value in decorative painting, 'imparting steadiness and artistic sobriety' to polychromatic schemes. Chocolate and chestnut browns are valuable and can be mixed well with white or black. Brown, when used in conjunction with blues, greens and other more assertive colours should not be too dark. Green–browns are highly valuable, especially when associated with greens in graduated colouring.

Purple.   Purple, the combination of red and blue, is seldom used, but makes an agreeable contrast with gold. It makes a good colour for dados and panels if mixed with brown.

Russet.   This deep and subdued colour is produced by combining red, yellow and blue, with red in excess. It is most useful in decoration and can incline either to purple, in which case its contrasting colour is deep green, or to orange, in which case it contrasts well with a subdued blue–grey.

Olive.   Olive is the tertiary colour formed from purple and green. It is of the greatest value in decoration, with a retiring quality. The antagonist or harmonizing contrast of olive is deep orange. It can be mixed in various proportions and also lightened by white.

Black and white.   These two colours, the extremes of the colour spectrum, are of limited though clearly defined use, in polychromatic decoration. White is sometimes used in small quantities, but rarely in its pure form.

Black forms an admirable ground for rich colours and gold. It is also used successfully to highlight the contours of joinery, such as on skirting, in combination with other subdued colours.

126

CHAPTER SIXTEEN

Wallpapers

THE ROMANTIC NOTIONS OF THE VICTORIANS, their love of flowers, birds, rich colours and heroic themes were evident in many aspects of their decoration. However, wallpapers, with their burgeoning bouquets, galloping garlands and fabulous festoons, were perhaps the most popular vehicles of sentiment. Papers called flocks, golds, satins, leatherettes, sanitaries and pictorials appeared in abundance in Victorian houses. They added texture, pattern, colour and general lustre to walls and ceilings. Combinations of friezes, dados, panels, borders and filling papers provided the special decorative effects so much enjoyed by the Victorians. Wallpaper in its many forms was probably the greatest single boon to decoration of the period.

From about the middle of the nineteenth century, the manufacture and use of wallpapers were revolutionized. Newly-evolved wallpaper machines disgorged volumes of paper destined to transform the abodes of rich and poor alike. In response to an eager, clamorous market, manufacturers created papers of greater diversity, complexity and ingenuity than ever before. Intensive effort went into design, production and finishing as papermaking became a huge industry.

The relatively rare and special hand-stencilled papers of the Georgian period were eclipsed by reams of colourful and elaborately designed Victorian papers. Hand-blocked papers, however, were not entirely superseded by the mechanized production. They held their own to some extent, as they still do today, being appreciated for their particular qualities by a small sector of the market.

Fantastic variety of design and abundance of choice made it possible for the first time in history for almost everyone to participate in the decoration bonanza. Even the humblest cottager could enhance a room with the new and wonderful wall-hangings which *Cassell's Household Guide* proclaimed:

The exceeding rapidity with which paper-hangings can now be produced, and their wonderful cheapness, have led to their adoption as a means of decorating walls, in preference to many other, and we are bound to say better, plans of effecting the same purpose. For instance no-one can doubt the superiority of the finely wrought tapestry which was hung in former times over the walls of those houses the inmates of which could afford such expensive luxuries; but upon the other hand, the walls of the humblest cottage may now be rendered cleanly and comfortable in appearance, at the cost of a few shillings. Upon the whole, perhaps, the greatest benefit to the largest number is the safest principle; and the popular style of wall decoration certainly brings with it this recommendation . . . that it is within the reach of all.[1]

Imitations became the rage. Almost any material, if sufficiently coveted, was regarded as a fair target for imitation. Silk, satin, velvet, tapestry and leather all succumbed to the indignity of being represented on paper, along with the rather unlikely choices of masonry, marble, timber, plaster and drapery. It was quickly realized by manufacturers and marketers that householders, especially of the expanding middle classes, desired to upgrade their appearances. They were ever-

Above: Potter and Company's sample book from Manchester, England, dated 1886. Papers shown are of the cheaper pulp variety, where the paper itself forms the background colour.

Fig. 7—Alabastine; dado and border, simple treatment. Fig. 8—for hand-painting. Fig. 9—Gothic dado and border. Fig. 10—Dado borders for stencilling over plain painted dados.

anxious to adopt for themselves any of the accoutrements of their social superiors that were brought within their grasp. In this competitive climate, the production of wallpaper imitations was bound to flourish, and flourish it did. In fact, the entire history of wallpapers is based on imitation, particularly of textiles. Nevertheless, it was in the nineteenth century that the cult of imitation reached its peak in wallpaper design.

A survey of the development of wallpapers reveals that the design of many of the basic motifs adopted by the Victorians derived from earlier imitations. Initially, wallpapers were devised during the sixteenth and seventeenth centuries to replace costly woven fabrics that had been used to adorn and insulate walls from mediaeval times. Renaissance motifs, emblems, cartouches (scrolls) and coats-of-arms, as well as some fruits and flowers, were favoured elements. Late seventeenth-century designs included formalized baroque patterns and pictorial scenes with borders relating to the printed cottons, tapestries and needlework pictures of the period. Gradually, the designs became more isolated from their source and appeared in the Victorian era as traditional patterns.

The eighteenth century contributed further to the range of simulations of attractive fabrics. Lustrous silk in all its forms was a favourite. Splendid flocks based on brocade patterns with a velvet-like texture were used in special rooms of grand houses. This established their desirability in Victorian eyes and they were copied enthusiastically. Suggestions of brocade, velvet, satin and leather followed. Some simple diaper patterns such as the fleur-de-lis, the star and the trellis evolved at this time to become the perennial designs. The stylistic diversity in the designs of wallpaper in the nineteenth century was therefore immense. To the basic repertoire of eighteenth-century designs, derived from Renaissance sources as well as traditional textiles, were added the special fancies of the period.

From the 1870s there was a marked expansion of the scope of design. William Morris and his friends did much to awaken an enthusiasm for simple elements of nature. Cottage plants and flowers rose to esteem as subjects worthy of the designers' attentions. An admiration for naturalistic motifs became a distinctive theme in all aspects of decoration. The more restrained sprigs and bouquets of the early Victorian period gave way to the flowing, swirling, seething floral designs later in the century. There was a desire to exploit the artistic design-potential of plants rather than simply to make a representation of them. Many beautifully organized, harmoniously coloured designs resulted.

Pictorial papers were another outcome of Victorian creativity. The French tradition of scenic papers was continued and adapted to embrace more everyday motifs. Nursery rhymes were very popular as were sporting subjects and designs commemorating special events, jubilees, battles and exhibitions. An interesting fragment of such a paper was recently uncovered at Black Rock, Victoria. It was a narrative nursery paper, *circa* 1856, showing episodes of Uncle Tom's Cabin.

The incisive dramatic style of Japanese art made its way quickly into wallpaper design. A powerful sense of geometry and simplicity can be seen in many designs of the last quarter of the century. Dados, which were usually based on a panel or other geometric form, were frequently given a Japanese flavour. From this exotic source came the sunflower and other distinctive motifs used in wallpapers.

An account of the range of paper-hangings exhibited in the Melbourne Exhibition of 1880 informs us of the standards by which wallpapers were judged. A concern for knowledge of 'decorative principles both past and present' reveals a basic preoccupation with the historic approach.

The exhibits in this class sent from Great Britain, Germany, France, and Austria, were such as to merit the highest commendation, being mostly distinguished by excellence of manufacture, beauty and appropriateness of design, and perfection of printing and finish. The knowledge and taste displayed in the exhibits show a thorough acquaintance with the principles of decorative art, both past and present. The higher class and expensive papers exhibited were fine specimens of the designers' art; whilst the purity, brilliance, and harmony of the colouring were such as to do ample justice to the reputation of the eminent firms exhibiting. In the cheaper goods, also, excellence of design and manufacture was shown . . . It is worthy of note that the extravagant and inappropriate floral arrangements so much in vogue with the paperstaining trade a few years ago, were generally absent, and that when flowers were introduced . . . it was with the correct taste and judgement. The great majority of the designs, however, were in conventional flowers and ornament in soft and gentle tints of harmonious colours.[2]

Production of wallpapers until approximately the middle of the nineteenth century was by the simple method of hand-printing. In England the first machine-prints were marketed in 1841 by C. H. and E. Potter although the French maker, Jean Zuber, had been producing them earlier. By the hand-printing method, a block of wood on which the design was carved, was pressed on to a sheet of paper after dipping it into a trough of colour. Until papermaking was industrialized, the sheets of paper were a standard 21 inches by 31 inches (about 55 centimetres by 78 centimetres). After printing they were pasted on the wall.

Of primary significance to the identification of wallpaper is the mode of manufacture. In the Victorian era, wallpapers were broadly divisible into two classes, hand- and machine-printed. Today to these are added silkscreen-printed papers and photogravure- and flexigraphic-printed papers. Hand- or block-printed papers show on the margin a register of the repeat of each block, whereas with machine-printing the pattern is continuous. Hand-printing has become a rarity, only being carried out by a few firms in England, the U.S.A. and France, Cole and Son of London being the chief English suppliers of historic papers.

Victorian manufacturers of both methods produced paper of great complexity, involving a high standard of technology and design. The basic principle of machine manufacture consisted then, as it does now, of a central cylindrical drum, from which the paper ran continuously. Numbers of smaller wooden rollers, sometimes as many as twelve, each bearing an element of the design applied in brass to its surface, were arranged around the central cylinder. The paper came off the cylinder, passed around all of the rollers in succession, and emerged fully printed at the end.

The practical advantage of hand-printing is that generally the matching of the paper is truer and the colouring more even. There is a tendency in machine-made papers for the paper to oscillate slightly, thereby producing some inaccuracy in the printing. Aesthetically, block-printing is perhaps more attractive than machine-printing, as hand-blocked papers tend to have a textural beauty as well as the colour and design components. The colours, applied one by one in rather heavy paints, build up a distinctive effect as they dry, whereas in machine-printing the colours are printed swiftly and thinly in one operation.

Apart from the distinction between hand-blocked and machine-printed papers, there were many different types and qualities of papers that appeared in Victorian houses. Each developed to satisfy a particular need or direction in the market. Many were in special classes emanating from particular makers. They make up a vast and varied panorama of styles and techniques.

The cheapest class of wallpapers are *pulps*, in which the natural colour of the paper itself, either as ground or ornament, forms part of the finished surface. Then there are *grounds*, in which the whole paper is coloured with a ground, preparatory to printing the design on it. *Satins* are papers in which the grounds are polished or glazed before printing. *Micas, golden frosted*, and *chrystal damask* are papers in which, while still wet, the grounds are powdered with talc or mica to produce a satiny sheen. The effect is rich and showy. *Embossed* papers are those in which the pattern is stamped in relief. Papers that are given an all-over texture in stamping are termed *grained* papers. *Sanitaries* were washable wallpapers printed in oil-colours on a heavily sized or otherwise prepared ground. The process for their

Gilbert and Sullivan operas form the motifs for this late Victorian wallpaper. Papers of a topical or commemorative nature were very popular.

Right: Among the rarest paper surviving in Australia is this one at Clairville near Launceston in Tasmania. It is one of the special panoramic papers or papiers peints made in France until about 1840. They were painted by hand, in small squares, generally depicting an historic event. There is no repetition at any point, the design forming a continuous scene. This paper celebrates the arrival of an important naval figure, possibly Napoleon, at Egypt in 1798.

Middle right: The beautiful drawing-room wallpaper at Navarre Station, Victoria, creates the impression of being made of fabric. Many wallpaper designs were copied from choice materials, such as velvet, tapestry and silk.

Far right: The popular story, Uncle Tom's Cabin, *is told in this rare and charming paper uncovered in fragments at Black Rock House, Black Rock, Victoria. The paper is* c. 1855.

Right: The cheapness of wallpapers meant that owners of simple timber cottages, such as this one, could afford a roll or two to decorate their rooms. The tug of fashion was, even in those circumstances, very strong, as can be seen by the use of the popular dado, filling and frieze formula. Note the paper around the door in lieu of an architrave (page 12).

Middle right: A typical mid-Victorian floral frieze survives at Runnymede near Hobart, a property of the National Trust of Australia (Tasmania).

Far right: Nursery papers were always in high demand in Victorian households. They frequently had a narrative theme.

This very grand English dining-room has a panelled arrangement of panoramic papers. The table setting and rather remarkable sideboard decoration are also interesting.

Assorted friezes and borders from the Victorian period.

production differed somewhat from the conventional method in that it used intaglio-engraved copper cylinders. Sanitaries became immensely popular not long after their introduction in 1884. A distinctive smoothness and muted colouring tended to typify them. *Sanitums* and *washables* as their names suggest were printed in a washable distemper and spirit colour insoluble in water. They did not have the glossy surface of the sanitaries. *Metal* papers were papers in which pattern or ground was printed in an imitation gold, metal or bronze powder. The paper in the billiard-room at Eynesbury is a good example of this type. *Golds* were papers in which gold leaf was used instead of imitations.

Flocks were made in three degrees of complexity. The intention behind all of them was to suggest velvet, either plain or printed, because it was such a highly favoured material. *Plain* flocks had the pattern or ground of finely shredded wool known as flock. This was made to adhere to the paper by printing in a strong gold size (glue) and dusting the flock over the size while it was sticky. *Heavy flocks* were subjected to flocking three or more times to build up the raised pattern to some 3 millimetres high. These were often used for painting and were therefore only printed in white. *Stamped* and relief flocks were printed with several flockings, but not from the same block, the relief being thus graduated. The pattern was afterwards stamped with hot dies with shaped relief. The plain flocks are still in production though the quality is, in most machine-made examples, reduced.

Imitation leather papers were made in great variety. Heavy stamped paper pulps were printed and then treated with metals, bronzes and lacquers in a variety of ways. *Varnished papers* were those sold already varnished. Most advice predicted a better result if the varnishing were done after hanging. Varnishing was used to increase the serviceability of papers, especially for hallways and stairways.

The dimensions of wallpaper were dictated by the size of the original paper sheets from which the earliest stencilled wallpaper was made, that is, Imperial size, which was 22 inches by 31 inches (53 by 78 centimetres). When these sheets were joined to make strips, a limit of twenty 22-inch width blocks, roughly 10 metres in length, was set. In Europe the traditional measurement was somewhat narrow, approximately 45 centimetres wide by 8 metres long. Friezes and borders were made of almost every width and were generally arranged so that one or more exactly occupied the width of the paper.

For the purpose of dating wallpapers it is interesting to note that from 1839 it was possible to register designs in England. From 1842 to 1883 a lozenge-shaped mark was used on the margin of the paper, giving code letters for the month and year. From 1884 designs were numbered. The Public Record Office in London is able to supply dates and other information for these marks.

The way the Victorians selected wallpaper for specific purposes is best understood in relation to particular rooms and their requirements. Certain conventions, however, did prevail and some papers did have a precise application. In particular, washable and sanitary papers were used in kitchens, offices, passageways and stairway dados. In bathrooms, housemaids' closets and sculleries, either a varnished paper or a sanitary paper was often used. Flocks were for good rooms where the presence of dust and gas did not spoil their appearance.

There was no more significant aspect of the manufacture of wallpaper in the Victorian era than reduction of cost. Throughout the nineteenth century, the cost of wallpaper fell, making it an extraordinarily popular commodity. Its availability facilitated a dramatic stylistic and social metamorphosis. The direction of change in interior decoration was largely influenced by the great volumes of highly decorative and inexpensive wall covering. Without such an accessible commodity, it seems unlikely that the decorative boom would have been so widespread and have had such profound social penetration. The notion of interior decoration as a vehicle for personal taste, which was so much the hallmark of the period, was brought about by many factors, but for the poorer classes especially, participation in the idea was made possible by cheap wallpapers.

CHAPTER SEVENTEEN

Floors and Floor Coverings

THE TREATMENTS OF FLOORS in Victorian houses varied as much as the treatment of walls and ceilings, and the decorative significance of the floor treatment varied considerably according to the status of the house and use of the room. Broadly, the chief materials used for floors were timbers, mostly softwoods, and the coverings were either carpet or linoleum and other related materials.

In the better rooms of grand houses, floor treatments became most elaborate: 'Those to whom expense is no object may have their floors of parquet; and very nice they are whether they extend all over the room and are merely covered by rugs in various places or whether the parquet is only used for bordering.'[1] The timbers used in the making of parquet floors were hardwoods, chosen for their variety of grain and colour to add a more ornamental effect to the floor. Labassa is an example of a grand house in which parquet was chosen for the floor in the main reception rooms.

Hardwoods, used sometimes in narrower widths, were also highly esteemed. Or softwoods such as kauri could be used in narrow widths to create a distinctive effect. If softwoods such as pine were used, which was most often the case, then they were enhanced with staining and varnishing. 'Good staining, with or without varnish, is perhaps next best [to parquet]'.[2]

In the rooms where floors were stained and generally varnished in this way, the main part of the floor was covered with a carpet square. These squares were made in regular sizes to fit rooms of a conventional size (that is about 3.6 metres by 2.7 metres or 3.6 metres by 4.5 metres). They allowed approximately 45 centimetres of stained boards to show around each side of the square. Their designs consisted of the main central position of the carpet known as the body and the outer band known as the border. Many carpets were made with these parts woven simultaneously. In others, the border was made separately and could be attached to a variety of body carpets. In a few rather select rooms, usually of an irregular shape, the carpets could be fitted all over, the border being shaped to fit the contours of the room. This is the closest the Victorians came to our modern concept of wall-to-wall carpet. They did not, however, adopt the associated principle of plain carpet overall, but preferred a patterned effect.

The convention was to have the carpet patterned in one of a variety of styles. Oriental designs provided the basic range of designs for carpets, which were machine-made in their thousands in the Victorian period. Turkey carpets were held to be the best for the dining-room, while the handsomest Aubusson and Axminster were favoured for the drawing-room. Many middle-class houses in England had hand-made carpets from the East. The ever-resourceful industrialists copied the designs precisely or made their own adaptations for machine manufacture. Very splendid carpets resulted.

Another popular field of designs was that of floral work. Elaborate designs with leaves, stems and flowers entwined were immensely successful in the general

Linoleum in the style of a carpet is used in this Queensland interior. An angora rug adds a little extra luxury to the room.

market. Passion flowers, chrysanthemums, lilies, roses and other floral favourites were seen to spring from the floor or to provide a gladelike garden through which one threaded one's way in moving around the room.

The same style of carpet, the patterned body and border, was used to carpet passages and stairs. The common narrow width was known as a runner. Runners were in standard use for stairways, where the carpet was held down at the base of each stair by a brass rod.

The chief alternative to carpet was the range of materials known as oilcloths. Their use began in England in the eighteenth century, the first reference to their fairly widespread acceptance as a floor covering being indicated by the inclusion of 'a large floor cloth' in the list of contents of the dining-room at Denham Hall in Suffolk.[3] Subsequent references show that they were used both as the principle floor covering in a room and as adjuncts to carpets. In some dining-rooms they were painted to match the carpet laid around them. Some householders considered them to be fresher and cooler than carpets and were therefore favoured for summer use and for use in warmer climates. This may well have increased their popularity in Australia, certainly in Queensland.

No. 5.—54 x 36, 46 x 27 and 36 x 24 inches.

No. 17.—54in. × 36in.

No. 4.—36in. × 24in.

No. 2.—46in. × 27in. and 36in. × 24in.

Geo. Harrison & Sons, Pattern Lithos., Bradford.

No. 21.—54in. × 36in. and 45 in. × 27 in.

No. 14.—54in. × 36in.

MATS.—A QUALITY.

Houses in India were far better adapted to the heat than those in Sydney, where English people chose to build English houses in an un-English climate, wrote Louisa Anne Meredith in 1844:

The only cool arrangement generally adopted is the substitution of an oiled cloth or matting for a carpet on sitting-room floors; some of the mattings are fine and rather pretty-looking, but the oiled cloth has always a kind of hair-dresser's-shop look about it. which not the most elegant furniture of every other description could reconcile to my old-world prejudices; and the noise which the softest step makes upon it is always unpleasant.[4]

Oilcloth is similar to linoleum, which succeeded it. It was made with a cloth backing, originally linen or calico, and an upper surface of oil-based material on to which decorative designs were painted or, in the nineteenth century, printed. The primary object of such designs was to imitate more costly materials, especially to give the effect of the illustrious hardwoods and mosaic floors. Other inspirations for designs were marblework and oriental carpets. A linoleum design made by the Corticine Company in England was 'Adapted from a Hunting Scene in a Carthaginian Pavement, 385 B.C.'.

The popularity of oilcloth was due mainly to its relative cheapness, since it cost approximately a quarter the price of carpet, but also to its practicality. While being decorative, it did not have the disadvantage of being susceptible to moths and other insects, and it was easily cleaned. Compared to carpet, it did not harbour dust or odours so readily. Therefore it became the standard Victorian floor covering for service areas as well as the chief substitute for carpet in lesser rooms or in less pretentious houses. Passageways, kitchens, sculleries, pantries, maids' rooms and similar rooms were ideally suited for its use.

In suburban houses with basements . . . kitchen sounds and smells . . . it is convenient to buy oil-cloth and have a border of it very carefully laid so as to exactly fit into all doorways, windows and corners. Oil cloth with the ordinary conventional patterns on it is unsuitable for this, but it is now made in very close imitations of oak and walnut and also in exact copies of parquet.[5]

Rippon Lea in Victoria has some interesting examples of floor treatments in its service regions. Linoleum runners in the Persian-carpet style with borders have been used on the back stairs and in passages. Terracotta tiles, another highly serviceable treatment, have been used in the basement, kitchen and storage areas.

Oilcloths were made in several forms and were sold under various names. Kamptulicon, a variety of oilcloth, is mentioned by Rocke as an ideal choice for the bedroom floor covering in front of the washstand. Another cheap material was coconut matting (coir), which was recommended for servants' rooms and similar areas.

There has been a small revival in the production of oilcloths for restoration purposes in the U.S.A. Patterns are created by hand-painting, stencilling and silk-screening. A brochure can be obtained from Floorcloths Inc., 109 Main Street, Annapolis, MD 21401.

Not everyone could afford timber floors. Earthen floors were used in cottages where timber floors would have been too expensive. According to Loudon, 'equal parts of lime, sand and cinder-dust, worked up well together, make very good . . . floors'. Clay floors, made of a mixture of clay and marl were used in England for floors in barns, hay lofts, malting houses and cottages.[6] Chopped straw 'well trodden by horses' was mixed in thoroughly and sometimes bullock's blood was added. A small cottage near Yandoit, Victoria, had, until recently, a highly serviceable earthen floor in its main room. The ceiling is lined with brown paper, while the walls are made of stone and mud with a rough plaster lining, which is white-washed.

CHAPTER EIGHTEEN

Stencilling

THE TECHNIQUE OF STENCILLING was a mainstay of decoration for centuries before the Victorians adopted it and made it such an extensive art. Some superb examples can be seen in the great Gothic churches of Europe. Vast areas of lofty walls are decorated with interconnected bands and panels of stencilled designs in beautiful colours. Of immense decorative interest are the rooms of Pompeii, which show simple geometric border designs stencilled above the dado. The Pompeiian rich reds, ochres and siennas were also adopted by some Victorian designers in their stencil work. Pompeii proved a rich field for the historically-minded designers of the eighteenth and nineteenth centuries. Early American decorative art reflects the European tradition of stencilling as a means of decorating humble houses.

Stencilling has flourished in the decoration of greater and lesser objects by simple folk and artisans alike. By its intrinsic simplicity as a technique it is adaptable to the widest range of decorative purposes. It is still quite viable today in its basic form using a limited number of colours.

In its simplest form, the monochromatic stencilled design calls for the least amount of technical expertise. A home-owner or everyday tradesman would be capable of preparing and applying the design. More complex designs involving two or more colours are the province of the skilled tradesman. The most elaborate stencilled decorative schemes, resembling murals more than applied decoration, are the work of highly skilled artisans. The subtleties here involved, in graduating colours to create a naturalistic effect, present considerable challenges.

The classical vocabulary of motifs and the Gothic decorative vista provided a rich range of designs from which the Victorians chose their many stencil designs. In fact, they saw few problems in adding to this already vast array by adapting motifs from any exotic source such as Japanese art. As a result, many original designs emerged, especially in the later years of the nineteenth century, in the wake of Whistler and the pro-Japanese designers in particular. In Victorian books on the art of stencilling, designs are grouped under headings such as Greek, Neo-Grec, Mediaeval, Japanese, Conventional Floral and Miscellaneous Ornament. Various coordinated designs for wall and ceiling decoration are shown in each category.

The Victorians devised many uses for their stencilled designs. They used them to enhance almost every architectural feature of an interior. Especially favoured were arches, ceilings, and the dados and friezes of walls. Bands and borders found their way on to some part of almost every significant room, unless their place was taken by wallpaper. The more elaborate the feature, the more elaborate became the mode of decoration. Modest cottages without the elaborate plasterwork of their lush middle-class counterparts used frugal monochrome borders to create dados and to emphasize the junction of wall and ceiling. Stencilling in most houses, except the most lavish, was confined to the major rooms only. Service rooms and maids' rooms usually warranted only a simple painted treatment.

A modest but effective stencilled border defines the top of the dado in this Queensland interior.

An 1882 photograph of Mintaro, Victoria, showing the high quality stencil work on the frieze and ceiling.

Far left: An excellent example of the beauties of stencilling, at Para Para, South Australia. Walls, ceiling and joinery have been richly stencilled.

Above: A highly decorative stencilled dado.

Top: Stencilling of a less pretentious style.

Top left: Very fine stencilling adorns a drawing-room ceiling.

Left: Detail of the dining-room dado of Para Para, at Gawler.

139

Plan of designs used in the decoration of a wall.

Plan for the stencilled decoration of a ceiling.

Public buildings relied considerably on stencilling for their interior beautification. Designers of government houses, town halls, prestigious government offices and other grand edifices found in stencilling a technique that could expediently cover their interiors with hand-painted, important-looking decoration. Some splendid examples survive and some impressive descriptions of the not-so-fortunate. Both serve to remind us of what beauties have been painted over or destroyed in work that was carried out on a splendidly generous scale.

Technically, there are two ways of transmitting a decorative design to a surface. The basic way is to cut a design out of stiffened, paint-repellant paper, sheet metal or plastic, one plate for each colour, and to paint through the cut-out sections. This is the method that is widely understood as stencilling. The alternative way is to prick a series of small holes around the outline of a design and then to dab the dotted outline, when it is in position, with a bag of coloured powder. When the sheet is lifted, the design will be shown in a series of dots on the wall or other surface. This is known as pouncing. The design can then be painted in with a free hand and brush. Of these two methods, the first is more widely used and is more straightforward for most circumstances. Pouncing, however, has its merits when a large complex design, more like a mural, is being transferred, in which case few repeats of any part are required. Pouncing enables a number of workmen to tackle a major project, piece by piece.

Once the design is transferred to the wall, there remains a choice: whether the colour is applied flat and uniformly in the more typical stencil method or whether the colour is broken or graduated. By the first method, which is most suitable when applied to geometric patterns, such as the frets (for example, Greek key), the colours are even and entirely distinct from each other. The effect is crisp and flat. By the alternative approach, a more naturalistic effect is achieved, and an added dimension is bestowed upon the work. Instead of fresh brushes being used for each colour, one brush is used and charged alternatively with two tones. Thus the colours run into each other and a more subtle effect is achieved. This technique is particularly suitable for naturalistic subjects such as leaves, fruits, figures, floral designs and scrolls that are painted in panels. It requires a far greater degree of skill in its execution than the straightforward one-brush, one-colour approach.

Wall patterns, whether in stencilled designs or wallpapers, can be grouped under two classes of ornamentation, namely diaper work and powdering. Diaper work includes all patterns that spring from some continuous feature or that repeat so closely together as to produce an even distribution of pattern and ground, thereby creating a uniform effect of colour. Powderings, on the contrary, show motifs of a distinct and independent nature, repeated at regular or (as is common in Japanese art) irregular distances, and not connected by any continuous feature. This distinction becomes important in the identification and selection of any wall design.

Victorian decorative artists stretched the technique of stencilling to its limits of impressiveness and scope. In their hands it became a remarkable art form capable of transforming an interior into a rich decorative entity. An enormous range of designs was evolved, from the simplest monochrome border used on plain painted walls in a cottage, to immense panoramas of angels, clouds, scrolls and entwined decoration that graced the ceilings and other surfaces of formal rooms in splendid houses and buildings.

Stencil work has a distinctive aura and impact. It has something of the charm of hand-painted work and the special visual appeal of repeated patterns. The beauty of the technique lies in its fundamental simplicity and its versatility. It commends itself for so many purposes, creating such an immediate impact for relatively little effort. It adds colour, definition and style, as well as enhancing architectural detail. It is probably the most easily reproduced of the Victorian decorative techniques, accessible to anyone prepared to observe simple rules and blessed with commonsense. In the absence of a complete range of Victorian wallpaper, stencilling is one of the best ways of creating a Victorian atmosphere in a room. It can also be used very effectively in combination with wallpapers.

How to stencil

1. Selection of a design

Ideally, when one employs one of the nineteenth-century decorative techniques, one does so in order to restore decoration that one knows was there originally. In such cases, careful examination of the evidence from all sources should be made in order to make every possible attempt to reproduce the design precisely as it was. The desire to modify the colours or any other aspect of the work should be resisted in the interests of authenticity. If the design has been painted over at some time, then patient scraping and soft sanding of the covering layers should reveal enough of the design for a tracing to be made. Often the only clue to original stencilling buried under paint is the faintly discernible raised design that shows under strong light projected at an angle. In Sydney, the restorers of the former New South Wales Club in Bligh Street achieved a magnificent result in the restoration of stencilling that had been obliterated by cream paint. Paint remover used with split-second timing can remove layers of paint from a stencilled design.

If evidence of original work is lost, it is necessary to find a substitute as close as possible to the original. As well as examining all physical and photographic evidence, the house itself and other similar houses should be scrutinized for all the designs they contain. Cornices, tiles, chimneypieces and other fixtures should give a lead as to the prevailing style. There must be a cohesiveness between the elements in each room and in the house generally. The one style of ornament should govern the decoration and furnishing of any particular room. Having established this, it then remains to choose an appropriate design from those available in the particular style of your house. Several books contain examples though few offer colour schemes. Time spent at this stage is well rewarded later on. Often it is necessary to alter the scale of the design, and this is not difficult. First, trace the pattern on to a sheet of paper and rule in squared lines of a reasonable size. For instance, a large design might require 6 centimetre squares, a small one about 1 centimetre. Make a second sheet with squares bigger or smaller by the required size-change. Then transfer the pattern free-hand, square by square. This can also be done by an enlarging machine.

2. Preparation of a stencil

First, you need to work out how many colours you will need and how the colours will divide, as a separate stencil will be needed for each colour. Many designs are quite successful if executed in one colour but often a greater interest is achieved by the use of two or three colours. Once this is worked out, the stencil designs can be drawn on to paper and cut out with a sharp knife, such as a Stanley knife. The paper used can be special pretreated stencil paper (available from art-suppliers) or any stiff-bodied paper. By traditional methods, ordinary heavy paper needs to be soaked in linseed oil for twenty-four hours and coated with Shellac to stiffen it and make it water-repellant. Alternatively, using modern materials, it can be coated with a polyurethane. Stiff plastic is also good and is already paint-repellant.

When multiple stencils are used, keys are needed on each stencil to properly position it in relation to the work that has already been executed. These keys are small cut-outs that allow you to see an identifying part that has already been painted. Paint is not applied through the keys.

Another important factor in making a stencil is the ties. The ties are the sections of paper that hold the pattern together on the stencil, that is, the portion of the design not cut out. Some stencils have a simple-enough design not to need ties to keep the stencil from falling apart. Others, with concentric circles and other

The traditional method for enlarging stencil designs. Designs are copied on to squared paper and then transferred to paper which has been squared according to the desired increase or decrease in size.

141

complicated elements, need supporting bands such as ties. Some show their ties in the executed design, revealing the means by which they have been applied. This easily identifiable 'stencilled look' is quite appealing but is generally confined to less ambitious work. Usually, the small parts under the ties are filled in by hand after the stencil is executed.

3.   Execution of the stencil

Having selected the appropriate stencil or copied an original one for restoration, and having prepared the actual stencil, the exciting time comes when it can be applied to the wall or other surface. In anticipation, the surface must be prepared as one would for painting, and chalk lines marked as guides above and below the line of work. Familiarity with the design and its arrangement on the wall is also necessary before beginning.

Paints used should be flat, oil-based or acrylic but heavy-bodied. The all-important question of colour must be planned carefully. Ideally, the colours should be those used originally, and precisely copied. But if a choice is necessary it should be influenced by what is appropriate to the style. The section on colour in Chapter 15 should be of assistance. It is often necessary to experiment to achieve the correct balance of colour. Practice does improve one's capacity to mix, complement and harmonize colours.

The other materials required are a stencil brush, which is squat and stubby, and some newspaper on which to wipe off excess paint from the brush. Preliminary practice with the stencil and brush on a hard surface should be done to develop expertise. The paint is applied through the holes by holding the brush in a perpendicular position to the work. The brush should be rather dry and the paint thick, otherwise the paint will dribble under the edge of the stencil and spoil the design. The motion of brushing can be either a gentle dabbing or a slight swirl of the bristles. Work out your own technique according to the requirements of the design. The degree of dryness of the brush is vitally important to the success of the .operation. A modern alternative to the brush is a small roller.

The base colour, or background of the design, can be applied if it is not the same colour as the general surface, and work can begin with the first stencil.

When one stencil has been executed around the room, the second or subsequent ones, if there are any, can be applied, using the keys to fix a spot each time the stencil is moved. If the design requires ties, you will have to decide whether they form part of the ultimate design or not. Flowing lines, scrolls and more complex designs should generally be made continuous by hand-painting the sections where the tie has been.

A final touch in most examples of bands and borders is provided by the parallel lines above and below the main design. These can be done, after some practice, by holding a long ruler at an angle to the surface and painting along the upper edge. Alternatively, lines can be ruled in chalk and the space between filled free-hand.

Below: A simple rosette, crudely cut out of a scrap piece of cardboard in 1896.

Bottom right: A frieze design, c. 1890.

Bottom: Example of a cardboard stencil, of a very simple design, used as a corner ornament, c. 1890.

CHAPTER NINETEEN

Wood-graining

GRAINING IS THE IMITATION of the natural veining, curl and character of woods. It is performed by first painting a thick ground colour, in strong oil-paint, a shade lighter than the general colour of the wood to be imitated. This is then covered with an opaque mixture of the appropriate hue and full depth, which is combined, streaked and lined with the contours of the grain being imitated. The treatment is completed by 'over-graining' and varnishing. In successful examples, the finished result is indistinguishable from the wood that has been imitated. Many examples, however, are merely suggestive of a particular timber, rather than being exactly like it. Some general work of average quality created only a look of timber rather than imitating a specific wood.

For the Victorians it was a marvellous technique, whereby inferior woods such as pine could be made to look like the rarer, more expensive woods such as oak, mahogany, walnut, birch, rosewood, satinwood, cedar and maple. In fact, any prestigious wood could be imitated on the surface of a more ordinary wood. Preferences for various woods differed widely according to local factors and fashions. The most common wood-graining in England and Australia was oak, with mahogany a close second, its special use being in offices and shops. Various sections of oak timber were imitated specifically. They were pollard oak, root of oak and dark oak. They were often used in combination with the basic straight grain or wainscot oak to give variety.

As a technique, wood-graining did not originate with the Victorians but was practised in waves of fashion from the baroque period through the Georgian and Regency periods, along with imitation marbling. After its rejection during the Palladian era, wood-graining was strongly revived in the last quarter of the eighteenth century. Examples of its use date from the late seventeenth century when the intention was not so much to deceive as to create an attractive textural novelty that could be admired and enjoyed.[1] Very splendid examples enriched grand houses, often covering the entire wall area in complex panel arrangements that combined marbling and gilding. Expediency of decoration was not a factor in such circumstances. The imitations were enjoyed for their own sakes, untainted by any overtones of pretension with which they were later associated. In 1836, Loudon wrote that all woodwork should, if possible 'be grained in imitation of some natural wood, not only with a view of having the imitation mistaken for the original, but rather to create an allusion to it and by a diversity of lines to produce a kind of variety and intricacy which affords more pleasure to the eye than a flat shade of colour'. He clearly saw the technique as a decorative treatment in its own right, to be appreciated for its own visual impact and for its contribution to the total effect of the room. The bogus factor, though acknowledged, was not the over-riding factor.[2]

Although wood-graining was baptised and blessed in the baroque period, in the full bloom of the Victorian era it rose to full stature as a decorative treatment.

Much controversy attended its popularity; nevertheless the fashion for wood-graining continued unabated. It became a standard treatment for joinery in houses, shops and offices.

Exclamations of horror came from Eastlake, who wrote in 1879: 'The practice of graining wood has not, however, been so long in vogue in this country as to command a traditional respect. It is an objectionable and pretentious deceit, which cannot be excused even on the grounds of economy.'[3] The imitative element in the technique disturbed many decorators, who saw in the decorative arts a reflection of general morality. To them the notion of overlaying one timber with a shallow imitation of another was abhorrent. The underlying social implications of such a falsity, were deplorable: 'the more cleverly it is done, the more absolute the untruth'.[4] But wood-graining was one of a rash of imitations indulged in by the Victorians. They used wallpapers that imitated almost everything, including cloth, leather, silk, plaster, marble and granite. And they loved silver plate and veneered furniture, which were in principle the same as wood-graining. So a welter of imitations confronted the moralists.

Supporters of wood-graining justified its use by saying that 'the imitation of Wood and Marble is always allowable where wood and marble would be employed by the Architect'.[5] Whatever the justification, its practice flourished. Wood-graining created an impressive effect at very little cost. It was possible for the appearance-conscious home-owner of any class to enhance his home quite considerably by this simple stroke. For as much as it cost to paint it, he could give his house the look of solid timber joinery. The traditionally illustrious and exclusive timbers such as oak and mahogany were brought within the reach of everyone, in appearance if not in substance. The Victorians had a happy knack of letting appearances suffice in many respects and decoration was an integral part of this facility.

Post-Victorian critics have ridiculed and deplored Victorian decoration and all its sham techniques. This is to fail to understand the decorative philosophy of the period and the real merits of treatments such as wood-graining. In rejecting the falseness, the merit of the decorative style of which it is a part is unrealized. One needs to immerse oneself in the aspirations of the age, in order to appreciate the joys of polychromatic colour-schemes, rich patterns and bogus elements such as lustrous wood-graining. Without sampling some of the Victorian enthusiasm for ornament and the pride in material and technical achievement, it is impossible to derive the full pleasure from Victorian decoration. Wood-graining and marbling are a fundamental part of the total fabric of decoration of the period.

Apart from the claim graining may have as a decorative finish, it commends itself considerably for its practicality. Grained surfaces are both durable and easily touched up. They do not show dirt and scuff marks as do painted surfaces and their vitality lasts much longer. Though the vogue for domestic wood-graining has waned, it is still used in hallways and other heavy-service areas in public buildings, especially in England. Many nineteenth-century houses in Paris still retain their wood-grained front doors for a combination of aesthetic and practical reasons.

In Australia most of the wood-graining of the nineteenth century has been obliterated. Few examples in public buildings remain and only a handful of domestic examples survive. Of these, Wardlow is an excellent example with the hallway and drawing-room joinery in wood-grained walnut. It is not a grand house but is rather more comfortable and middle class in its tone. Wood-graining suits it perfectly. From this and other similar examples, it is possible to estimate the extent of the use of wood-graining in Victorian houses. The majority of middle-class terraces and villas in Victorian houses in Australia would have used wood-graining as a decorative treatment. Suburbs such as Brighton, Hawthorn and Parkville of Melbourne, Balmain, Paddington and Glebe of Sydney, and North Adelaide, would have abounded in examples of wood-grained splendour.

As a decorative treatment for joinery, wood-graining would have been supreme among the middle class in suburbia.

As with most Victorian decorative techniques, the degree of skill required in the execution of wood-graining is not essentially very great, although some practitioners demonstrated a more marked flair than others. Any respectable firm of decorators would have carried out graining and marbling, as well as paper-hanging, painting and stencilling. Advertisements proclaimed: 'Plain & Fancy Painting of every description, including, Gilding, Bronzing, Staining, Graining, Marbling, Varnishing, Polishing, Kalsomining and Paper-Hanging'. Proponents of the art of wood-graining claimed that it 'required, in spite of much that has been said, a degree of taste, observation and dexterity of hand that places this art in rank far above that of plain painting'.[6] Practice, however, was probably the indispensable factor after the mastery of the basic technique.

Practical instructions in books, manuals and articles were widely available. Titles such as F. B. Gardiner's *Everyman His Own Painter* (1872), W. J. Pierce's *Painting and Decorating* (1892) and J. Petrie's *The Practical Arts of Wood-Graining and Marbling* (c. 1886) were among the range of books available on the practical aspects of wood-graining.

Stage 2 of oak wood-graining. Section by section the areas are worked while the mixture is still wet.

Today the expertise is in the hands of a few skilled, traditionally trained tradesmen. A fine example of recent work can be seen at Tasma Terrace, the Melbourne offices of the National Trust of Australia (Victoria). A return in popularity of the technique would no doubt see a re-emergence of tradesmen able to practise it.

Wood-graining was applied to joinery rather more often than to furniture. Doors, architraves and skirting boards were especially favoured for graining. Some examples combined the imitation of two or more woods, as somewhat of a feature, on doors in particular. The example illustrated, Westella, has 'maple' set in panels of a 'walnut' door.

Middle-class home-owners revelled in the beauty of their wood-grained entrance halls and front rooms, while the more affluent saw it only as a reasonable enhancement for the plainer service areas. Distinctive solid timbers or polychromatic paintwork were generally chosen as joinery treatments for their prestigious front rooms, in preference to the ubiquitous wood-graining. Labassa is a fine example of the preference for complex painted treatments and solid blackwood joinery rather than wood-graining. Mandeville Hall has painted joinery in the drawing-room and bedrooms, and solid oak panelling in the dining-room. However, the dining-room's doors and architraves are wood-grained. The execution is so excellent that the difference is barely discernable.

How to wood-grain

Instructions on the technique of wood-graining in the nineteenth century range from a one-paragraph synopsis for the handy-man, to a massive treatise on the art of wood-graining for the professional. Similarly, there is a wide range in the quality of work, every grainer having his own style and trade secrets. Individual formulas for the graining coat, in particular, abound. If you are interested in doing your own graining, experimentation and practice will make it possible to achieve that which, at the outset, seems highly technical.

The treatment consists of three basic stages of application:

(a)	the base coat, which is a semi-gloss oil-paint of the colour slightly lighter than the lightest colour of the wood imitated.

(b)	the opaque graining coat, which usually consists of pigment in an oil base but which can be water-based.

(c)	the thin, opaque over-graining coat, which is usually water-based and lends an extra depth to the work.

(d)	the varnish coat.

145

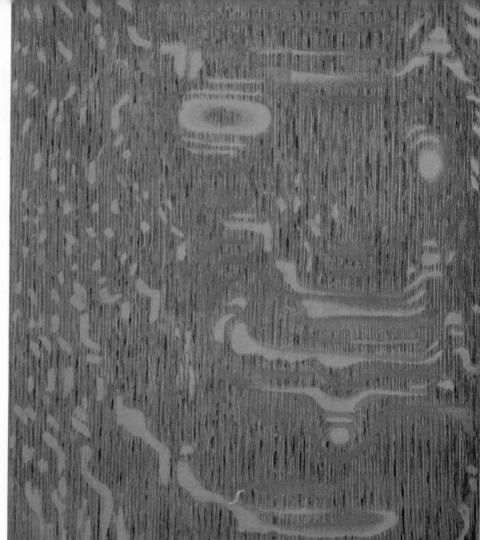

Above: Stage 1 in the graining of oak. The ground colour shown at the base is applied first in semi-gloss oil-paint. Then the graining mixture is applied and combed.

Above right: Stage 2: the knots and variations in the grain are worked, usually by holding a blunt flexible instrument, such as the end of a comb, under a rag. Alternatively, a strong thumb nail can be used.

Right: A successful example of wood-graining in imitation of mahogany is shown here at Pastoria, Victoria.

Far right: Contrasting two types of wood-graining was an effective decorative practice. This example shows bird's eye maple in the panels, and oak in the stiles.

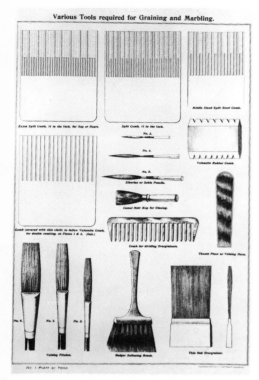

The various tools required for graining.

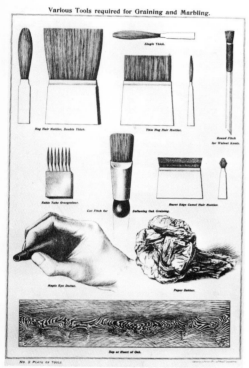

Further tools required for graining.

Sometimes the over-graining is omitted or carried out after the first varnishing where there are two coats of varnish. Each additional coat adds depth to the finished work. However, it is possible to achieve a successful result with only the base coat, the graining coat and varnish.

As oak is the most commonly imitated wood, the steps in wood-graining of that timber are outlined here, though the principles are applicable to all graining and only the particular pigments and graining strokes vary from wood to wood.

Oak wood-graining

1. The base coat

After thorough preparation of the surface to be grained, it should be painted with a semi-gloss oil-paint in a warm, yellowish-cream colour, a fraction lighter than the lightest shade in a piece of golden oak. Berger paints make a colour called toffee, which is a good standby if you are not going to mix your own colour. The paint must be semi-gloss or it will not take the working of the graining coat which follows.

2. The graining mixture

The graining coat is essentially a thin coat, with an opaque quality something like diluted treacle. Only a relatively small quantity of mixture is required as it covers very sparsely. It is generally prepared with a base of approximately equal parts of boiled linseed oil and turpentine, but some grainers use a water-based mixture that dries rather quickly.

The traditional oil-based mixture is made as follows: Melt a small piece of beeswax in a little linseed oil, mix in the graining colours (available from art-suppliers) that is, equal parts of yellow ochre, burnt sienna and raw umber, and thin the mixture with turpentine. The beeswax has the effect of slowing down the drying process a little to enable the graining to be done. It also gives body to the mixture so that the various lines of graining do not run together. Some recipes mention a megilp or grainer's cream which is a substitute for the simple beeswax. This mixture is made either with a beeswax base or a soft soap base to which are gradually added turpentine and oil. In effect, the megilp gives the mixture a jelly-like consistency.

Strain the mixture before applying it and stir it often. If the mixture appears to set too quickly, before it can be conveniently worked, add a small amount of boiled oil. If it runs too freely, add some of the melted beeswax or megilp. If the colour is too light, add more umber; if it is too dark, add more oil and turpentine.

3. Graining tools

The graining tools need some introduction. Traditionally, the grainer uses a range of metal combs with teeth of different spacing and a number of brushes with specific properties. However, considering the relative rarity of these pieces of equipment and the varying extent to which they were used by individual grainers, the list is reduced to the minimum, and some improvisations are suggested.

First, one must have a thin, flat brush known as a flogger. It is important in preparing the graining coat for combing and veining and in some types of graining it is used to create a range of effects.

The basic range of steel combs used by the professional grainer consisted of at least three sizes with teeth of varied spacing. It is important to have at least one of these combs in metal or in some substituted material such as leather or cardboard. The main one has simple, evenly-spaced square-ended teeth and is easily replicated. The split comb has every second tooth absent and the teeth are narrower.

For the stage after the combing, a piece of equipment is required to mark in the veins. Individual grainers use either their own thumb-nail, a piece of horn shaped like a thumb-nail or the corner of an ordinary plastic comb. What is really required is a rounded, blunted edge in a firm but not hard material. Whatever is used is wrapped in a soft rag to allow it to clearly wipe out the marks without leaving hard edges.

For the over-graining, a loose, long hog-hair brush that leaves a small amount of soft marking on the already grained surface is required. If the actual brush is unavailable, a similar sort of brush like a wallpaper brush should be used.

To add to this array of basic equipment, there are some other tools that are curious enough to be mentioned. They are the various roller-grainers, which emerged in response to the need for more and more rapid wood-graining. They were neat little rollers usually with the graining pattern incised on them. Some combined a brush with a roller and others provided an appropriate finish. They were probably efficient and reasonably effective, if predictable in their results.

4. Applying the graining mixture

The graining mixture can now be applied to a small area of the surface, assuming that some practice has been carried out on a spare board. The mixture should be brushed on evenly, sparingly and in the direction of the timber. A very important point is the formation of the junctions of panels in the wood. They must be clearly defined, even a little emphasized.

5. Graining

With a clean, dry, flat brush go over the surface evenly, removing any excess of mixture. This brush is known as a flogger and can be used to complete the graining treatment if a different effect from the combing is aimed at. If the flogger is used sideways to streak the mixture, it results in a smooth effect. However, used conventionally, the flogger is used prior to the combing.

6. Combing

Using the basic comb, the work is gone over in straight lines in the direction of the grain. All junctions and panelled effects should be observed carefully. The end of the comb should be wiped frequently to keep the lines clear. Some grainers do this combing with a soft rag over the comb which softens the marks a little. Then the comb, or a split comb if you have one, is run over the work but in a deviating direction. As the path of the second comb crosses that of the first, it creates an effect of the pores or actual grain of the wood. The comb should be twisted in the hand as it is moved along the work, crossing in broad diagonal sweeps of approximately seventy-five degrees to the first combing. This may sound difficult but, in fact, is easily grasped in practice.

Careful observation of the actual timber being imitated enables one to understand the purpose of the combing process. Allow a slight build-up of the mixture at the junction of panels, stiles and rails as this enhances the finished work.

7. Further graining

After combing, the marking of the broader veins is done while the work is still wet. This is called 'wiping out of the lights' or 'putting in of the champs or clashes'. It is this stage that is the most challenging in wood-graining. The subtleties of the technique emerge. First, not all the sections of work should have the veins marked out. Either the panels, such as on a door, are selected for veining, or the stiles and rails. This variation of treatment serves to consolidate the structural effect of the door. The areas on which it is carried out must also somehow relate to each other and a consistency of effect must be evident. The swirls of one panel should be balanced on an opposing panel. Here it is most important to have studied real wood and wood-graining in order to have an image of the grained panel and the whole work in the mind's eye. Practice also enables one to mark the veins with just the right degree of deliberateness, an almost casual naturalness. The movement is an almost trembling swirl, sideways to the first combing. If the markings are too stiff the effect will be disappointing and if they are too flowery they will be overpowering. So there is the challenge.

The spaces between these marks are then mottled to show the undulations of the grain, and the shadows that lie side by side with the light markings and any little touches or softening necessary to complete the likeness to the wood are put in.

After completing this entire graining stage on one section another can be started. Work proceeds in this way, section by section, until the whole job is finished.

8. *Over-graining*

After the grained surface has dried, the over-graining can be done. Usually the mixture consists of colour, ground in water. A little blue–black with or without burnt umber gives the basic pigment. To this is added stale beer or a little milk to bind the colour and then the mixture is thinned with water to a mere wash. It is then laid on with the over-grainer so as to represent the general light and shade, in mass, of the wood. Over-graining gives depth to the finished work which is desirable but not always essential. Whether or not one over-grains is a question of how much trouble one is prepared to go to in achieving the appearance of real wood.

9. *Varnish*

When all the work is finished, section by section, and over-grained, the whole can be varnished in either a gloss or semi-gloss varnish. Modern polyurethane, though suspect to some people, seems to me to be a valid substitute for old-fashioned varnish, which is hard to obtain and tricky to apply.

To wood-grain in imitation of other woods, it is necessary to vary the base-colour and the graining mixture as well as some of the graining techniques and tools used. After oak, the most widely grained wood is mahogany.

Mahogany graining is not considered as difficult as oak, and is usually done in water-colour. The ground colour is a warm beige consisting of a venetian red and burnt sienna with a little ochre. The graining colour is deep red brown, a mixture of rich vandyke brown and a little blue–black. The tools used are a thick hog-hair mottler, a sponge, a short camelhair mottler, and a badger softener. The graining colour is laid on and manipulated into form with a sponge and the mottlers, and then softened and lightly flogged with the side of the badger softener to produce the fine grain of the wood. The over-graining is done with a thin fitch-hair over-grainer using vandyke brown in water.

Walnut is another popular wood, and is grained in both water-colour and oil. For the ground, use yellow ochre and burnt sienna. For the graining mixture use burnt umber and vandyke brown, or burnt sienna and a little blue–black. After painting in the ground, the graining mixture can be applied sparely, and with a wet leather 'wipe out the lights' and mottle in the way that the light and dark parts of the wood occur.

After this dries, use a fitch and an over-grainer to put in the main markings and knots. Touch it up with a soft rag and the badger softener. Then put in finer veins with a sable pencil and blend together frequently. Finally, over-grain with a separated over-grainer, which is like six artist's brushes side by side.

CHAPTER TWENTY

Marbling

MARBLING AND WOOD-GRAINING are closely linked in Victorian decoration as the predominant imitative techniques. They often appeared side by side, joinery having been wood-grained and plaster and timber chimneypieces marbled. Entrance halls in particular were often marbled, giving them a rich quality. The practice of marbling, however, began earlier than the nineteenth century. Along with wood-graining, elaborate forms of marbling had been executed at least as far back as the latter half of the sixteenth century, a fact which is generally overlooked by critics of the falseness of Victorian decoration. Sometimes entire walls were divided into panels of varying dimension that carried a range of marble types, in complex geometric arrangement.

Cornforth and Fowler's book, *English Decoration in the Eighteenth Century*, includes some splendid examples. One, the parlour at Stanton Harcourt Parsonage, Oxfordshire, is amazingly elaborate. The fields of the panels on doors and walls imitate walnut veneer, the mouldings are marbled green; the stiles imitate porphyry; the skirting and chimneypiece imitate purple marble. So the Victorians had a solid precedent on which to base their extensive use of imitative techniques.

In the nineteenth century many uses were found for this technique. Marbled columns and scagliola, which was a composite imitation marble, were favoured especially in entrance halls and large reception areas. They formed a powerful element in the internal architecture of many grand buildings, both domestic and public. Large wall spaces were also devoted, as in the eighteenth century, to panels of various imitation marbles.

A splendid example of this treatment survives in England at Brodsworth Hall in Yorkshire. The work was completed in 1868. Vividly contrasting panels of red, green and yellow marble cover the walls of the stairwell. The staircase rises steadily along the wall, while tall white marble pilasters ascend in two tiers, from the stairs to the ceiling.

In Sydney, at Elizabeth Bay House, a small fragment of green marbling was found on an archway leading into the oval hall from which the staircase rises. During the recent restoration of the building the full archway of green marbling was restored.

A superb example of marbling is to be seen at Mintaro in Victoria. Fluted Corinthian columns in imitation of rich yellow sienna marble stand upon impressive square bases of reddish-brown marbling and are flanked by yellow marbled pilasters. The skirting is of deep green marbling streaked with white. The entire composition of variously coloured marbling lends great style to the entrance hall.

The other application of marbling was in transforming relatively modest fittings in houses into rather more impressive ones. In this way smaller houses could mimic some of the glamour of bigger houses. By imitating the real marble

Imitations abound in this picture of the entrance hall at Mintaro, Victoria. The skirting is of green marble over plaster, while the columns are in sienna marble on a red and grey coloured base. The dado is stencilled, as is the illusory dado rail.

of a fine house, a worker's cottage could be greatly enhanced. Simple wooden chimneypieces could be marbled to good effect. From a distance, no-one could tell the difference between the simulated marble and actual marble and all agreed it looked better. The best rooms of cottages had chimneypieces marbled in this way. So did the main rooms of slightly larger houses and the lesser rooms of grand houses. The practice of imitation was embraced from the bottom rung upwards, throughout the ranks of society, a fitting use being found for it at all levels. Instructions were given in books for specialist painters and general tradesmen and marbling was part of the training of painters and decorators.

One can generalize about the process of marbling but in practice there are many individual ways and secrets followed by specialists in the techniques of graining and marbling. The basic principle is the same for both techniques. The painter works up from a ground colour, which relates to the predominant colour of the material being imitated. The ground is usually somewhat lighter than the general colour. Thus a grey marble would be grounded in very light grey and the figuring and veining worked in grey, black and white. This working can be done in either an oil-colour or water-colour. For the latter, beer is often used as a medium, and a confident hand is necessary, as the mixture dries quickly and the working must be done while it is still wet.

All instructions stress the need to follow the natural example and to practise the techniques thoroughly. To work any specimens of marble, a little knowledge is required of the nature, character, division of ground and principal parties or masses in the marble. The chief pitfalls for the marbler are over-working, which leads to an undistinguished result, and 'flatness' caused by a failure to emulate the way in which the veining of marble comes through in different planes. Close observation of an actual sample usually prevents this happening. The end result should have a lifelike vitality and crispness.

How to work sienna marble

Finally, as an example, let us look at instructions for the working of sienna marble, a much-favoured marble of rich yellow and brown colouring. In its typical form, it consists of irregular and angular pieces of a strong character. In some specimens, it is intermixed with tints of broken red, deep yellow and white intersected by dark veins, along which it usually breaks.

The instructions and accompanying illustrated stages of work are derived from *The Practical Arts of Wood-graining and Marbling* by J. Petrie.

To carry out the work, the following materials and equipment will be needed:
(a) a range of colours mixed rather thick in raw linseed oil and turpentine, that is, a small quantity of deep yellow (oxford ochre or raw sienna), purplish-brown (a mixture of two-thirds victoria lake and one-third prussian blue), reddish-brown (venetian red or burnt sienna) and some white;
(b) a badger-hair softener (that is, a very soft brush), a fine pointed brush and several ordinary small brushes.

Stage 1

The first step is to apply at least two coats of white paint as a base. While the top coat of white is still wet, dab on the thinned yellow mixture, in patches. Follow with the red mixture greatly thinned in other patches. Take care that the red mixture does not become too dominant. Wipe off dribbles with a sponge. Then with the badger-hair softener, soften the patches together. The result should resemble the Stage 1 illustration.

Stage 2

With the purplish-brown mixture, put in some broad and fine veins in the same direction as the patchy tints, using a fine pointed brush. Use the badger-hair softener as you go to blend the veining in with the ground. Otherwise the veining

may look harsh and superficial. Leave some veins more distinct than others. It should now resemble the Stage 2 illustration.

Stage 3

Mix up separately on the palette some rich red (raw sienna) and red–brown (burnt sienna). This will be used to further develop the veining. Firstly, carefully put a few touches of the red inside the different blocks or parties, some of them larger than others, varying them as much as possible. Then, using the other brush and colour from Stage 2, fill in a few of the smaller blocks. Similarly, put in a few light touches of white, between the fine veins. Then soften all the work.

Finally, make a dabber out of rolled-up paper as in the illustration of tools and dip it first into turps and then into white paint, and then lightly dab it on to the palette to make the mixture more even. Then go over the work, dabbing systematically and lightly, taking care to achieve a consistent result, as in the Stage 3 illustration.

Stage 4

When the work described above is dry, a few darker touches of the dark brown can be put in between the small and large blocks. Also some fine lines of the darkest lake veining colour can be put in over those previously laid on. The same colour, greatly thinned, can be put in some of the open spaces, softened as before.

A good effect may be achieved by passing a few thin yellow veins across different parts of the work, in an opposite direction to the existing veins. A few thin white transparent veins can also be made to run over the work in various directions, care being taken not to make them too prominent. The finished result can be seen in the Stage 4 illustration. When the working is completed and dry it can be protected by varnish or a thin coat of beeswax.

There are many marbles that can be tackled by this approach. Overall, a certain depth and appearance of density should be aimed at, a solid quality that typifies marble. The softening, which is so important, ensures that the various veins appear to float up through the marble rather than sit flat on the surface.

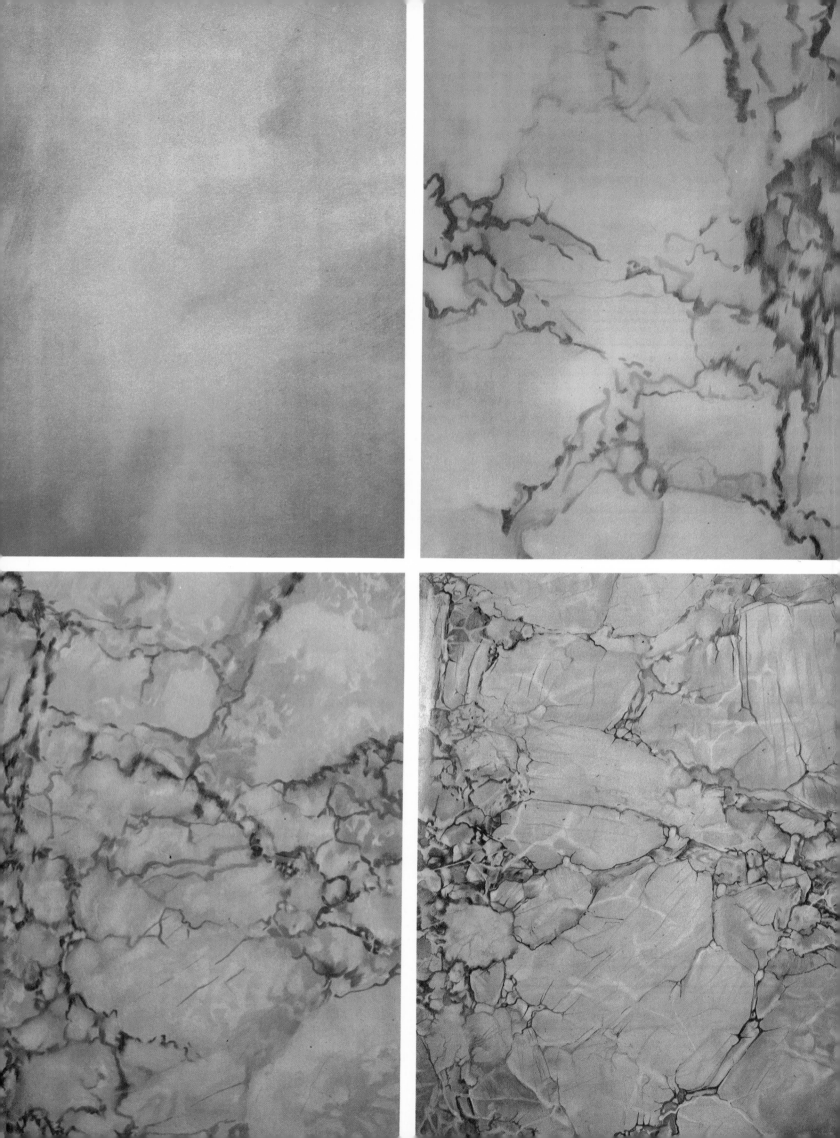

Left: An unsophisticated example of marbling at Rouse Hill House, New South Wales.

Middle left: Stage 2. Some broad and fine veins are put in. The work is softened again with a badger and repeated.

Far left: Stage 1 in the imitation of sienna marble. A thin ground of base colour is applied and daubed in patches with thinned white paint. It is merged in with a badger softener or equivalent.

Left: A detail of the wall treatment in the entrance hall of Yallum Park, South Australia, shows an oak wood-grained skirting with a marbled wallpaper dado carrying an overprint that suggests a stencilled border.

Middle left: Stage 4. Using the dabber soaked with thin whitish mix all the work is gone over again. (See full instructions page 152.)

Far left: Stage 3. A few touches of deeper colour are put in inside the different blocks, or parties, some of them larger than others. The work is softened again and some fine whitish patches added.

Glossary

architrave   Decorative timber moulding surrounding a window or doorway.

cast iron   Iron, moulded into forms, often decorative. Not to be confused with wrought iron.

chimneybreast   Projection on a wall, accommodating the flues and the fireplace.

chimneypiece   Surround to a fireplace. Made of marble, timber, plaster or cast iron. (Generally called a mantelpiece.)

cornice   An ornamental moulding running around the wall of a room, generally where the wall joins the ceiling. Also the ornamental projection within which curtains are hung—nowadays called a pelmet.

coffer   A recessed panel in a ceiling, vault or dome.

closet   A small room fitted up to serve as a privy, or an iron or porcelain pan furnished with water supply to flush.

cartouche   Ornament in the form of a scroll.

ceiling rose   Ornamental centrepiece for ceiling, below which the light fittings hang. Usually made of plaster.

door furniture   Door knob, finger-plate or escutcheon on door.

dado   Any lining, papering or painting of the lower part of an interior wall, approximately one-third of its overall height, rendering it different from the upper part. Described as the foundation space of the wall.

diaper   An all-over design, in which the elements are linked by continuous lines, as in most wallpaper and stencilled decoration.

embossed wallpaper   Heavy pressed paper, which has a raised design, often imitating plaster, stone or leather.

encaustic tile   Decorated with patterns in differently coloured clays inlaid with the tile and fixed in a kiln and used for decorative treatment of floors, especially in hallways.

etched glass   Glass on which decorative patterns have been produced by the action of hydrofluoric acid. A similar effect is achieved by sand-blasting or grain-blasting.

eclectic decoration   That which borrows from various sources.

filling   Main area of the wall between *dado* and *frieze*.

frieze   A band of decoration painted, stencilled, papered or carved. Found on interior walls, above the *dado* or below the *cornice*.

fretwork   Decorative panels, usually of timber, from which portions have been cut away. Fashionable in late Victorian houses.

gas bracket   A gas light with one or two burners fixed to the wall.

gaselier   The central light of a room usually consisting of several branches, each with a burner and shade.

graining   A painting technique whereby cheaper softwoods are made to appear like the more highly prized timbers.

lavatory   Receptacle for washing hands. Generally called a wash-basin.

motif   A particular element in a decorative scheme and often repeated for general effect.

marbling   A painting technique whereby timber or plaster is made to resemble one of the various types of marble.

panel   Recess part of door or wall, often painted with special decorative designs or colours harmonizing with *stiles* or surrounding surfaces.

powdering   Designs in wallpaper and stencilwork of a distinct and independent nature repeated at regular or (as in Japanese art) irregular distances, not connected by any continuous feature.

runner   A strip of carpet or linoleum used in passageways or stairs, usually with a border design.

skirting   Board placed around the bottom of the wall of a room.

soffit   Horizontal face of *architrave*, beam or arch.

stile   Main areas of a door or window, often treated in a different manner from *panel* to achieve decorative interest.

swag   An ornamental festoon of flowers, fruit and foliage caught up at the sides and sagging in the middle. Created in various materials, also used in drapery.

valance   In decoration, any down-hanging drapery on a window, bed, and so on.

window furniture   Latches or other fittings—brass or porcelain—on windows.

Notes

Introduction
1 C. Daly, 'L'Amérique à la recherche d'un procédé de délassement,' *Revue Generake de l'Architecture et des Travaux Publics*, ser. 4, vol. 10, 1883, p. 83.
2 C. Dresser, *Studies in Design*, London, (n.d., c. 1874), p. 9.
3 R. N. Wornum, The Exhibition as a Lesson in Taste, in *The Great Exhibition—London 1851*, p. xxi.
4 E. Sutherland, quoted in W. H. Rocke, *Remarks on Furnishing and House Decoration*, Melbourne, 1874, p. 38.
5 Dresser, op. cit., p. 10.
6 D. Jones, *The Grammar of Ornament*, London, 1856.
7 M. D. Conway, *Travels in South Kensington*, London, 1882, p. 186.
8 *Cassell's Book of the Household*, vol. 1, London, 1889, p. 143.
9 A. Wells, 'Decoration', *Building, Engineering and Mining Journal*, 5 May 1892, p. 186.
10 W. Morris, *Some Hints on Pattern Designing*, London, 1899, p. 30.
11 *Beautiful Britain*, Chicago and London, 1894, p. 189.
12 C. Eastlake, *Hints on Household Taste*, London, 1878, p. 52.
13 Wells, op. cit., p. 186.
14 Conway, op. cit., p. 203.
15 R. Twopeny, *Town Life in Australia*, Melbourne, 1883, p. 34.
16 Wells, op. cit., p. 186.
17 Twopeny, op. cit., p. 30.
18 Rocke, op. cit., p. 6.
19 Twopeny, op. cit., p. 39.
20 ibid, p. 31.
21 Twopeny, op. cit., p. 44.
22 Rocke, op. cit., p. 18.
23 Twopeny, op. cit., p. 40.

Chapter 1: The Drawing-Room
1 'Beryl', 'Art in the Home', *Illustrated Sydney News*, 6 March 1890.
2 W. J. Loftie, *House Decoration*, Art at Home series, London, 1878, p. 28.

3 ibid., p. 29.
4 L. Orrinsmith, *The Drawing-room*, Art at Home series, London, 1877, p. 4.
5 R. Twopeny, *Town Life in Australia*, Melbourne, 1883, p. 40.
6 W. H. Rocke, *Remarks on House Furnishing and House Decoration*, Melbourne, 1874, p. 17.
7 ibid., pp. 18–25.
8 ibid., p. 26.
9 ibid., p. 27.
10 ibid., p. 31.
11 ibid., p. 44.
12 ibid., pp. 40–6.
13 M. Terry and P. Oakden, *What to Build and How to Build It*, Melbourne, 1885, p. 56.
14 A. Wells, 'Decoration', *Building, Engineering and Mining Journal*, 5 May 1892, p. 186.
15 'Beryl', 'Art in the Home', *Illustrated Sydney News*, 25 May 1890.
16 ibid.

Chapter 2: The Dining-Room
1 W. H. Rocke, *Remarks on House Furnishing and House Decoration*, Melbourne, 1874, p. 29.
2 C. Dickens, *Dombey and Son*, London, 1878, p. 382.
3 W. J. Pearce, *Painting and Decorating*, London, 1878, p. 8.
4 ibid.
5 A. Wells, 'Decoration', *Building, Engineering and Mining Journal*, 5 May 1892, p. 186.
6 ibid.
7 Rocke, op. cit., pp. 29–33.
8 R. Towpeny, *Town Life in Australia*, Melbourne, 1883, p. 43.
9 ibid., p. 45.
10 ibid., p. 46.
11 'Beryl', 'Art in the Home', *Illustrated Sydney News*, 17 April 1890.
12 ibid.

Chapter 3: The Entrance Hall
1 Sir Arthur Helps quoted in W. H. Rocke, *Remarks on House Furnishing and House Decoration*, Melbourne, 1874, p. 41.
2 W. J. Pearce, *Painting and Decorating*, London, 1898, p. 7.
3 ibid.
4 R. W. Edis, *Decoration and Furniture of Town Houses*, London, 1881, p. 45.

Chapter 4: The Library
1 J. Dyer (1758) quoted in W. H. Rocke, *Remarks on House Furnishing and House Decoration*, Melbourne, 1874, p. 39.
2 W. J. Pearce, *Painting and Decorating*, London, 1898, p. 9.
3 ibid., p. 39.
4 ibid., p. 40.

Chapter 5: The Billiard-Room
1 M. Girouard, *The Victorian Country House*, Yale, New Haven and London, 1979, p. 34.

Chapter 6: The Bedroom
1 W. H. Rocke, *Remarks on House Furnishing and House Decoration*, Melbourne, 1874, p. 43.
2 W. J. Pearce, *Painting and Decorating*, London, 1898, p. 9.
3 ibid., p. 9.
4 Rocke, op. cit., pp. 44–9.
5 R. Twopeny, *Town Life in Australia*, Melbourne, 1883, p. 43.
6 ibid., p. 45.

Chapter 7: The Kitchen
1 R. Kerr, *The Gentleman's House*, London, 1864, p. 227.

Chapter 8: The Bathroom
1 R. Kerr, *The Gentleman's House*, London, 1864, p. 227.
2 R. Twopeny, *Town Life in Australia*, Melbourne, 1883, p. 36.
3 *Cassell's Book of the Household*, vol. 1, London, 1879, p. 128.
4 Twentyman and Askew, Architects' Drawings and Specifications, Picture Collection, Latrobe Library, Melbourne.

Chapter 10: Mandeville Hall
1 E. M. Robb, *Early Toorak and District*, Melbourne, 1874, p. 100.
2 'A Habitable House', *Australasian*, 10 August 1878, pp. 166–7.
3 ibid.
4 *Melbourne Punch*, 7 January 1904.
5 ibid.
6 'A Habitable House', op. cit.
7 ibid.
8 ibid.
9 ibid.
10 ibid.
11 ibid.
12 A. Barker, in Ian Grant (ed.), *Great Interiors*, Spring Books–Hamlyn, London, 1971, p. 219.
13 'A Habitable House', op. cit.
14 ibid.

Chapter 15: An Approach to Restoration
1 'A Dissertation in the Dado', *Work*, 13 February 1892, p. 1.
2 'On Colour Applied to Form', ibid., 29 June 1891, p. 209.

Chapter 16: Wallpapers
1 *Cassell's Household Guide*, London, (n.d., c. 1880).
2 D. Donaldson, 'Paperhanging', in *Official Record of the Melbourne International Exhibition Catalogue 1880*, p. 81.

Chapter 17: Floors and Floor Coverings
1 *Cassell's Book of the Household*, vol. 1, London, 1889, p. 127.
2 ibid, p. 128.
3 J. Cornforth and J. Fowler, *English Decoration in the Eighteenth Century*, London, 1974, pp. 216–17.
4 Mrs C. Meredith, *Notes and Sketches of New South Wales*, Ringwood, Vic., 1973, p. 128.
5 *Cassell's Book of the Household*, op. cit., p. 127.
6 J. C. Loudon, *An Encyclopaedia of Cottage, Farm and Villa Architecture*, London, 1836.

Chapter 19: Wood-graining
1 J. Cornforth and J. Fowler, *English Decoration in the Eighteenth Century*, London, 1974, p. 190.
2 J. C. Loudon, *An Encyclopaedia of Cottage, Farm and Villa Architecture*, London, 1836.
3 C. Eastlake, *Hints on Household Taste*, London, 1878.
4 J. Petrie, *The Practical Arts of Wood-graining and Marbling*, Manchester and London, 1886, p. 9.
5 L. Orrinsmith, *The Drawing-room*, Art at Home series, London, 1877, p. 41.
6 Petrie, op. cit., p. 8.

Bibliography

Books

Audsley, W. A. and O. A., *The Practical Decorator*, Glasgow, 1892.

———, *Polychromatic Decoration*, London, 1882.

Barry, J., *Designs of Linoleum*, Kirkcaldy, Scotland, 1889.

Basher, Lady Mary, *The Bedroom and Boudoir*, Art at Home series, London, 1877.

Beautiful Britain: The Scenery and Splendours of the United Kingdom, Chicago and London, 1894.

Burke, Keast, *Gold and Silver*, Heinemann, Melbourne, 1973.

Byron, Joseph, *Photographs of New York Interiors at the Turn of the Century,* Dover, New York, 1976.

Cannon, Michael, (ed.), *Victoria's Representative Men at Home*, Heritage, Melbourne, 1978. First published *Melbourne Punch*, 1903.

———, *The Land Boomers*, Melbourne University Press, 1966.

———, *Land, Boom and Bust*, Heritage, Melbourne, 1972.

Cassell's Book of the Household, 3 vols, London, 1889.

Cassell's Household Guide, London, (n.d., *c*. 1880).

Cassell's Lady's World, London, 1888.

Clark, Fiona, *William Morris Wallpapers and Chintzes*, Academy Editions, London, 1973.

Conway, M. D., *Travels in South Kensington*, London, 1882.

Cooper, Nicholas, *The Opulent Eye*, The Architectural Press, London, 1976.

Cornforth, John and Fowler, John, *English Decoration in the Eighteenth Century*, Barnie and Jenkins, London, 1974.

Cox, Philip and Lucas, Clive, *Australian Colonial Architecture*, Melbourne, Lansdowne, 1978.

Corticine Floor Covering Co., *Sample Designs*, London, 1886.

Crouch, J. and Butler, E., *Apartments of the House*, London, 1900.

Cuffley, Peter, *A Complete Catalogue and History of Oil and Kerosene Lamps in Australia*, Pioneer Design Studio, Lilydale, Vic., 1973.

Daly, Cèsar, *L'Architecture Privèe due 19.me Siècle*, 3 vols, Paris, 1864.

Davidson, R. (ed.), *Historic Homesteads of Australia*, vol. 1, Cassell, Sydney, 1969.

———, *Historic Homesteads of Australia*, vol. 2, Cassell, Sydney, 1977.

———, *Historic Houses of Australia*, Cassell, Sydney, 1974.

Davison, Graeme, *The Rise and Fall of Marvellous Melbourne*, Melbourne University Press, 1978.

Day, Lewis F., *Ornament and Its Application*, London, 1904.

———, *Nature in Ornament*, London, 1892.

Dickens, Charles, *Dombey and Son*, London, 1878.

Downing, Andrew J., *The Architecture of Country Houses*, New York, 1853.

Dresser, Christopher, *Studies in Design*, London, (n.d., *c*. 1874).

Durant, Stuart, *Victorian Ornamental Design*, Academy Editions, London, 1972.

Eastlake, Charles L., *Hints on Household Taste*, London, 1878. Reprinted Dover, N.Y., 1978.

Edis, R. W., *Decoration and Furniture of Town Houses*, London, 1881.

Entwisle, E. A., *Wallpaper: Its History and Appreciation*, London, 1954.

Evans, Ian, *Restoring Old Houses*, Macmillan, Sydney, 1979.

Facey, James W., *Elementary Decoration*, London, 1882.

Freeland, J. M., *Architecture in Australia: A History*, Cheshire, 1968.

Gardiner, F. B., *How to Paint Your Victorian House*, American Life Foundation Library of Victorian Culture, New York, 1978; facsimile of *Everyman His Own Painter*, New York, 1872.

Garnett, Thoda and Agnes, *Suggestions for House Decoration*, Art at Home series, London, 1876.

Gillon, Edmund V., *Victorian Stencils for Design and Decoration*, Dover, N.Y., 1968.

———, *Decorative Frames and Borders*, Dover, N.Y., 1973.

Girouard, Mark, *The Victorian Country House*, revd ed. Yale, New Haven and London, 1979.

Grafton, Carol B., *Victorian Cut and Use Stencils*, Dover, N.Y., 1980.

Grant, Ian (ed.) *Great Interiors*, Spring Books–Hamlyn, London, 1971.

Great Exhibition—London 1851, catalogue, facsimile ed. Bounty, N.Y., 1970.

Greysmith, Brenda, *Wallpaper*, Macmillan, New York, 1976.

Heal and Co. Catalogue, London, 1853–1934.

Haldane, Robert, *Household Receipts*, London, 1883.

Holly, H. Hudson, *Modern Dwellings and Country Seats*, New York, 1863; reprinted 1 vol., American Life Foundation, New York, 1977.

Haweis, Mary E., *The Art of Decoration*, London, 1881.

Hay, David R. *A Nomenclature of Colours*, 2nd ed., London and Edinburgh, 1846.

———, *The Laws of Harmonious Colouring Adapted to Interior Decorations*, London and Edinburgh, 1847.

Hunter, George L., *Decorative Textiles*, Philadelphia and London, 1918.

Jennings, Arthur J. *Paints and Varnishes*, Pitman, London, 1919.

———, *Wallpaper Decoration*, The Trade Papers Publishing Co., London, 1907.

Jones, Owen, *The Grammar of Ornament*, London, 1856; facsimile edition, Van Nostrand, New York, 1972.

Kerr, Robert, *The Gentleman's House*, London, 1864.

Kirkcaldy Linoleum Company, *Linoleum Designs*, 1889.

Korner and Co., *Lamp and Bronze Ware Samples*, Berlin, 1879.

Lewis, Miles B., *Victorian Primitives*, Greenhouse, Melbourne, 1978.

Loftie, Martha J., *The Dining-room*, Art at Home series, London, 1878.

Loftie, William J., *House Decoration*, Art at Home series, London, 1878.

Loudon, J. C., *An Encyclopaedia of Cottage, Farm and Villa Architecture*, London, 1836.

Meredith, Mrs C. *Notes and Sketches of New South Wales*, London, 1844; reprinted Penguin, Ringwood, Vic. 1973.

Moreland, Frank A., *Practical Decorative Upholstery*, London and Boston, 1890.

Morris, William, *Some Hints on Pattern Designing* (a lecture delivered 10 December 1881), London, 1899.

———, *Wallpaper Samples*, 2 vols, London, (n.d., *c.* 1884).

Noetzi, C., *Practical Drapery Cutting*, Batsford, London, 1906.

Nylander, Jane, *Fabrics for Historic Buildings*, National Trust for Historic Preservation, Washington, 1977.

Official Record of the Melbourne International Exhibition, Melbourne, 1880.

Orrinsmith, Lucy, *The Drawing-room*, Art at Home series, London, 1877.

Pearce, W. J., *Painting and Decorating*, London, 1898.

Petrie, J., *The Practical Arts of Wood-graining and Marbling*, Manchester and London, 1886.

Potter, Alexander and Margaret, *Interiors*, John Murray, London, 1957.

Racinet, A. C. A., *L'ornament Polychrome*, 3 vols, Paris, 1885.

Robb, Emily M., *Early Toorak and District*, Melbourne, 1874.

Robertson, E. Graeme and Craig, Edith, *Early Houses of Northern Tasmania*, Georgian House, Melbourne, 1966.

———, *Victorian Heritage*, Georgian House and Ure Smith, Melbourne, 1960.

Rocke, W. H., *Remarks on Furnishing and House Decoration*, Melbourne, 1874.

Seale, William, *Recreating the Historic House Interior*, American Association for State and Local History, Nashville, U.S.A., 1979.

———, *The Tasteful Interlude*, Praeger, New York, 1975.

Shanks and Co. Sanitary Appliances, Glasgow, (n.d., *c.* 1892).

Smith, George, *The Cabinet maker and Upholsterer's Guide*, London, 1836.

Smith, John M., *Ornamental Interiors*, London, 1887.

Strong, Ray, Binney, Marcus and Harris, John, *The Destruction of the Country House*, Thames and Hudson, London, 1974.

Talbert, Bruce, *Victorian Decorative Arts*, U.S.A., 1876; reprinted American Life Foundation, New York, 1978.

Terry M. and Oakden, P., *What to Build and How to Build It*, Melbourne, 1885.

The Housewife's Treasury of Domestic Information, London, 1877.

Twentyman and Askew, Architects' Drawings and Specifications, Picture Collection, La Trobe Library.

Twopeny, Richard E. N., *Town Life in Australia*, Melbourne, 1883; reprinted Penguin, Melbourne, 1973.

Van Der Burg, A. R. and P., *School of Painting for the Imitation of Woods and Marbles*, London, 1878.

Walsh, J. H., *Domestic Economy*, London, 1856.

Ware, Dora and Stafford, Maureen, *An Illustrated Dictionary of Ornament*, George Allen and Unwin, London, 1974.

Wornum, Ralph N., 'The Exhibition as a Lesson in Taste', in *The Great Exhibition—London 1851*; facsimile ed., Bounty, N.Y., 1970, p. 1, Appendix 4.

Yapp, G. W., *Art Industry, Furniture, Upholstery and House Decoration*, London, 1877.

Zander, W., *Moderne Decorations Mallerein*, Berlin, (n.d., *c.* 1888).

Newspapers and Journals

'Beryl', 'Art in the Home', *Illustrated Sydney News*, 6 March 1890; 3 April 1890; 17 April 1890; 1 May 1890; 12 June 1890.

Brown, W. W., 'The Principles of Decorative Art, Historically and Practically Considered, *The Illustrated Carpenter and Builder*, 28 April 1886, p. 275; 30 April 1886, p. 299; 7 May 1886, p. 307; 14 May 1886, p. 331; 21 May 1886, p. 347; 28 May 1886, p. 363; 4 June 1886, p. 380; 10 June 1886, p. 395; 18 June 1886, p. 410.

Duncan, Dorothy, 'A Choice Assortment of Paper, Hangings for Sale by the Subscriber, Association for Preservation Technology, vol. 7, no. 2, 1975, p. 74.

Flaherty, Carolyn, 'Early American Wall Stencilling', *The Old House Journal*, vol. 3, no. 1, January 1975, pp. 1 and 8.

Flaherty, Carolyn, 'Drapes and Curtains', *The Old House Journal*, vol. 2, no. 4, April 1974, p. 1, p. 6.

Jennings, George, 'Illustrated Bathroom Exhibition', *Town and Country Journal*, 8 November 1879, p. 885.

Labine, R. A. 'Selecting the Best Floor Finish', *The Old House Journal*, vol. 3, no. 1, January 1975, p. 5.

Parsons, Frederick, 'A Dissertation on Wall Dadoes', *Work*, 13 February 1892, p. 753.

———, 'Modern Wall Coverings', *Work*, 19 December 1891, p. 415.

———, 'On Colour Applied to Form', *Work*, 29 June 1891, p. 209.

Wells, Andrew, 'Decoration' (lecture Sydney Architecture Association), *Building, Engineering and Mining Journal*, 5 May 1892, p. 186.

Welsh, F. S. 'Methodology for Exposing Wood graining', *Association for Preservation Technology*, vol. 8, no. 2, 1976, p. 71.

'Interior Decoration', *Building, Engineering and Mining Journal*, 15 June 1889, p. 442.

'Painting and Papering', *Work*, 23 January 1892, p. 715.

'Private House Decoration in Melbourne', *Australasian Sketcher*, 5 June 1880, p. 119.

'Stencilled Decoration for a Drawing room', *Work*, 28 March 1891, p. 217.

'The Diningroom of the Melbourne Coffee Palace', *The Weekly Times*, 16 September 1905.

'Tynecastle Tapestry: Designs for Ceilings, Friezes and Panels', *Illustrated Carpenter and Builder*, 19 February 1886.

'A Habitable House', *Australasian*, 10 August 1878, p. 166–7.

Sources of Illustrations

Page 13 (middle): Mr & Mrs W Kelleher; page 16 (third from top): Mr & Mrs R Roydes; page 17 (second from top): University of Melbourne Archives; page 20 (below): James Archer, Gracemere; page 20 (top): Charles Cullis-Hill; page 21 (top): Diana Allan; page 21 (below): Bert Weston; page 24 (top & below): State Library of Queensland; page 25: State Library of Queensland; page 28 (top): Charles Cullis-Hill; page 28 (middle & below): State Library of Queensland; page 29 (top): F W Niven Album, University of Melbourne Archives; page 29 (middle & below): State Library of Victoria; page 32 (top): University of Melbourne Archives; page 32 (below): National Trust of Australia (New South Wales); page 33 (below): Phyllis Murphy; page 33 (top): University of Melbourne Archives; page 36: State Library of Victoria; page 40 (top): State Library of Victoria; page 52 (top): State Library of Victoria; page 52 (middle): Charles Cullis-Hill; page 53 (top & below): State Library of Victoria; page 56 (top): State Library of Victoria; page 56 (below): University of Melbourne Archives; page 57 (top & below): State Library of Victoria; page 60 (top & below): State Library of Victoria; page 61: University of Melbourne Archives; page 64 (top & below): State Library of Victoria; page 65 (all photographs): State Library of Victoria; page 68 (below): State Library of Queensland; page 72: State Library of Victoria; page 76 (below): National Library of Australia; page 77 (below): John Morris; page 78 (below): Ken Turner; page 80 (all photographs): Ken Turner; page 81: Ken Turner; page 99 (top right & below): National Trust of Victoria; page 105 (all photographs): Loreto Convent, Marryatville; page 108 (all photographs): Loreto Convent, Marryatville; page 109 (all photographs): Loreto Convent, Marryatville; page 117: University of Melbourne Archives; page 128: Arthur Wigley; page 130 (top): Timothy Hubbard; page 132: Diana Allan; page 137 (top): State Library of Queensland; page 137 (below): Derek Rea; page 142 (all photographs): Richard McDonald.

Index